THE
LEGISLATIVE UNION
OF
ENGLAND AND SCOTLAND

THE
LEGISLATIVE UNION
OF
ENGLAND & SCOTLAND

THE FORD LECTURES

DELIVERED IN HILARY TERM, 1914

By P. HUME BROWN, M.A., LL.D.

FRASER PROFESSOR OF ANCIENT (SCOTTISH) HISTORY AND PALAEOGRAPHY IN
THE UNIVERSITY OF EDINBURGH
HISTORIOGRAPHER-ROYAL FOR SCOTLAND

GREENWOOD PRESS, PUBLISHERS
WESTPORT, CONNECTICUT

Originally published in 1914
by The Clarendon Press, Oxford

Reprinted from an original copy in the collections
of the Brooklyn Public Library

First Greenwood Reprinting 1971

Library of Congress Catalogue Card Number 70-114483

SBN 8371-4776-X

Printed in the United States of America

PREFACE

A NATURAL reason for my choice of the Legislative
Union of England and Scotland as the subject of
the Ford Lectures was its common interest for both
countries. At the present epoch, moreover, the Union
of 1707 may be said to have a direct and special
interest. The problem which the statesmen of the
reign of Queen Anne had to solve has close analogies
with the problem which has confronted their successors
in recent years. I did not consider it within my scope
to suggest these analogies, which, indeed, cannot be
missed in any presentment of the circumstances in
which the union of the English and Scottish Parliaments was effected. Neither has it been my object to
draw any specific lessons for the present from the
past. Identical problems do not recur in human
history, and each age has to find the solution of its
own. If the study of the past, however, does not
afford direct guidance for the present, it may have its
own influence on the temper and attitude of mind with
which existing problems are approached.

Another consideration influenced me in the choice of
a subject. Within the last few years the publication
of contemporary documents, hitherto unused, has
thrown fresh light on the characters and actions of the
leading Scottish statesmen of the time, as well as on

the general conduct of affairs. Most important of these are the *Papers of the Earl of Mar and Kellie*, published by the Historical MSS. Commission in 1904. Mar was Secretary of State for Scotland from 1705 till the accession of George I, and his voluminous correspondence is the most vivid and continuous record of affairs relating to Scotland which we possess for the period they cover. The *Seafield Correspondence from 1685 to 1708*, edited for the Scottish History Society by Mr. James Grant (1912), is mainly concerned with family matters, but it also contains letters which throw new light on certain public events, as, for example, on the invasion of 1708 in the interest of the elder Pretender. Of special value is the correspondence of John, second Duke of Argyle, which appears in the first volume of *Intimate Society Letters of the Eighteenth Century*, edited by the Duke of Argyll (1910). Argyle presided over the Scottish Parliament as Royal Commissioner in 1705, and his letters written from Edinburgh to Godolphin supply additional information regarding the state of parties at the time and his own relations to the English Ministry and his Scottish colleagues.

Besides these recently published materials I have made much use of unprinted documents in the British Museum and in the Record Office, London. Among these I may specially note the letters of John, Duke of Atholl, who held the office of Lord Privy Seal; of James Johnstone, Lord Clerk-Register; and of William, Marquis of Annandale, President of the Privy Council and Secretary of State for Scotland, most of which appear in the appendices. Even more important is the correspondence of James, Earl of Seafield, Lord High Chancellor of Scotland, which extends over the whole period, but is of special value for the session in which the Treaty of Union was carried in the Scottish Parliament. Seafield's letters are too numerous to be printed in an appendix, but the Scottish History Society has arranged for their publication in one of its volumes.

I should perhaps add that in a few statements of fact I have repeated what I have written elsewhere, as there seemed no necessity for expressing them otherwise.

I have to acknowledge my great obligation to Mr. R. K. Hannay, M.A., Curator of Historical Manuscripts, General Register House, Edinburgh, for his kindness in reading my proofs.

CONTENTS

LECTURE I

THE POLITICAL STATE OF SCOTLAND AT THE ACCESSION OF ANNE

LECTURE II

PROSPECTS OF UNION

Contents

LECTURE III

THE ACT OF SECURITY

Contents

LECTURE VI

THREATENED UNDOING OF THE UNION

xii   *Contents*

LECTURE I

THE POLITICAL STATE OF SCOTLAND AT THE ACCESSION OF ANNE

I

IN his dedication to his *History of the Union of Great Britain* De Foe characterized that event as 'the greatest and nicest concern' of his age, and the course of European history since his day has justified his opinion. For England the union of her Parliament with that of Scotland ranks with the Norman Conquest as a determining fact in her history. If the Norman Conquest made England, the union of the two Parliaments made Great Britain, for the union of the Crowns created no bond either of hearts or of interests. In the history of Scotland the only event of like importance was her acquisition of Lothian in 1018, by which she extended her bounds from the river Forth to the river Tweed, and thus became the kingdom which the world knows. And not only for England and Scotland, but for the nations of the Continent the Union of 1707 was an event of the first importance, and the English statesmen who were most directly concerned in effecting it were fully aware of the fact. 'But we are now in so critical a position . . .' wrote Godolphin to the Scottish Lord Chancellor Seafield, 'that all Europe must in some measure be affected by the good or ill ending of the Parliament of Scotland[1].'

[1] *Seafield Papers*, Hist. MSS. Com., Fourteenth Report, App., Part III, p. 199.

Had the Union not taken place when it did, the course of European history must have been materially different from what it has actually been. 'That England', writes my colleague, Professor Lodge, 'emerged victorious in the long duel which fills the eighteenth century, was due to many causes ; but not the least of these causes was the fact that England had been merged in Great Britain.'

Be it said that the period of his national history of which the Union is the central event is one that a Scotsman must regard with mingled feelings, among which pride is not predominant. For an Englishman, the same period is among the most glorious in his annals. Alike in the arts of war and peace England then shone pre-eminent, and the names and characters of the men who illustrated them are among the most familiar to English-speaking peoples. But to speak of glory in connexion with Scotland in the reign of Queen Anne would be mockery. What names has she to put over against those of Marlborough, of Somers, of Swift, of Addison, of Sir Christopher Wren ? Her constellation did not rise till half a century later. There were indeed Scottish statesmen of the time who by their gifts and accomplishments would have taken a foremost place in any deliberative assembly, but even to their own countrymen they are dim and ill-defined figures, barely existent in the national memory. Even for educated Scots, when not specially interested in history, the one definite fact is, that the reign of Anne saw the end of a Scottish Parliament, and, though they may consider it, on the whole, a beneficent event, they have a vague idea that it was not a very creditable transaction. Of the men who were mainly responsible for carrying out the transaction they have a misty conception that they were a somewhat questionable set. They have probably heard of Fletcher of Saltoun as the almost solitary incorruptible Scot of his time, and as the credited author of the saying that ballads are more potent things than laws; of Lord Belhaven as the Scottish Demosthenes who harrowed the feelings of his countrymen by his picture of the woes that must inevitably follow the loss of their national Council. The Duke of Argyle they probably know better as the good providence of Jeanie Deans than as one of the chief instruments in effecting the Union, and the Duke of Hamilton is probably known to them, not as one of its chief opposers, but as the great gentleman whose tragic end balked the ambition of Beatrix Esmond.

How are we to explain this ignorance on the part of Scotsmen generally of one of the most fateful periods in their national history? One reason naturally suggests itself. No shaping mind of a contemporary produced such a picture of his time as would permanently stamp its characters and its events on the mind of posterity. Speaking of the *Memoirs* of St. Simon, Sainte-Beuve remarks that they have made comparatively obscure every period of French history before and after that which they treat. Such a chance happened in the case of one age in the history of Scotland—the mid-period of the sixteenth century. In John Knox's *History of the Reformation in Scotland* we have the presentment of the chief events and actors of his time by one who had in eminent degree the powers which Emerson ascribes to Carlyle—'the devouring eyes and the portraying hand'. Momentous as were the events of that period, had Knox not written his book, our image of them would be many degrees paler than it is. For the succeeding periods we have not another Knox, but we have at least a measure of compensation. In the voluminous histories of Calderwood and Spottiswoode—the one setting forth the Presbyterian, the other the Episcopalian conceptions of the relations of Church and State—we have a detailed narrative of events which at least presents a coherent sequence. So for the reigns of Charles II and James VII, Wodrow's *Sufferings of the Church of Scotland*, largely made up as it is of original documents, puts us in closest touch with the period it covers. No such valuable compilation exists for the reign of William III, and in the national memory of that reign only two events persist—the tragedy of Glencoe, and the disaster of Darien. In the case of Anne's reign we are somewhat better off. In the copious *Memoirs* of the Jacobite Lockhart we have the record by a contemporary of the principal events of the time, written by one who was in the thick of what he narrates, and who, moreover, was both a keen observer and a caustic writer. But Lockhart's *Memoirs*, valuable though it is as a chronicle of the time, does not rank among the books that give an extrinsic interest to the subjects which they treat.

That the reign of Anne, therefore, is a comparatively obscure period of Scottish history is partly due to the fact that no great contemporary writer has made it live for us. But it has to be added that the story of the reign is not for Scotsmen an attractive one in itself. It is a period when human nature certainly does not appear at its best. This is not to say that its principal actors were naturally more depraved than men of other times and countries. But the conditions, public and private, under which they played their parts, were of a nature peculiarly fitted to try civic virtue.[1] What these conditions were we shall see as we proceed. Here it is sufficient to remark that a people does not gladly turn its eyes to a period when its representative men, whether from their own natural failings or as the result of temporary circumstances, compromise the national character in the eyes of the world. So it is, perhaps, that by a kind of unconscious instinct Scotsmen have averted their gaze from a reign so momentous in their country's destinies, and abounding, moreover, in men of striking gifts and individuality.

It was indeed a period which, by reason of the interests at stake, necessarily evoked the elemental passions of human nature. The questions that had to be settled concerned the very being of the State, and division of opinion regarding them involved concealed or open war. Open war did not come, but more than once in the course of the reign it was only accidental circumstances that averted it. But, if actual war did not arise, the words and actions of many of the leading persons of the time were those of men who regarded their adversaries not as political opponents but as

---

[1] The poverty of Scottish public men was one occasion of temptation. A journey to London, and a six months' residence there, was reckoned to cost £600, and it is stated that only one Scottish peer could meet the expense out of his own pocket. The Earl of Rosebery, a keen Unionist, accepted his appointment as one of the Commissioners for the Treaty unwillingly, on the ground that 'considering the scarcity of money in this country, it is not very convenient for me'.

enemies of the State against whom all weapons were permissible.

II

There is one governing fact of the period which must ever be in our minds as we follow the course of its events. It was a sense of the insecurity of the existing régime. In a certain measure this same sense of insecurity existed in England, but in Scotland it was an urgent preoccupation of the nation throughout the whole of Anne's reign. ' I am sorry,' wrote Viscount Dundee to a correspondent in the opening months of William's reign, ' I am sorry your Lordship should be so far abused as to think that there is any shadow of appearance of stability in this new structure of government these men have framed to themselves.' [1] The opinion so confidently expressed by Dundee was continuously present to the minds of Scottish statesmen during William's reign, but in the reign of his successor new conditions pressed it home with intensified urgency. While William reigned, it was known that Anne, a representative of the exiled house, would succeed him. But, as Anne would have no direct heir, who was to come after her ? All parties remembered that the Stewarts had once before been driven from their inheritance, and that both Scotland and England found that they could not do without them ; and they were recalled. In view of the irreconcileable divisions of the existing parties, was it not a probability that it might be found necessary to revert to them again ?

And actual events of the reign were such as to

---

[1] *Letters of John Graham of Claverhouse* (Ban. Club), p. 70.

deepen this national sense of the instability of the existing government. On the accession of Anne, the first thoughts of the Scottish Privy Council, as we shall see, were turned to the need of guarding against rebellion and foreign invasion. In 1708 there was an actual attempt at invasion in concert with the disaffected elements in the country, and every year, both before and after 1708, a similar attempt was regarded as a probability. And if the imminent threat of another revolution kept the nation in suspense and disquiet, the hopes and fears of it were ever-present motives in the action of public men. As their conduct is revealed in the correspondence of many of them, we see the shiftiness and indecision of men who meant to find their feet in any contingency.

Another cause of the wavering or tortuous action of public men was their uncertainty regarding the relative strength of the opposing parties in the country. No sure means existed of ascertaining how the nation would be divided in the event of revolt and invasion. General elections afforded no sure data, since the government of the day had always effectual means of influencing their results in its own favour.[1] It was, therefore, only on the vague assertions of interested persons that English Ministers could depend for information regarding the general feeling of the country. Hence, in the correspondence of the time we find the most contradictory statements regarding the relative numbers of those who were for and those who were against the Revolution settlement. On this uncertain

[1] For an illustration of the methods by which elections were conducted in Scotland see the letter of a candidate to the Earl of Seafield in the *Seafield Correspondence* (Scot. Hist. Soc.), p. 441.

information public men spoke and acted. The Duke
of Hamilton and others, for example, both in their
public and private utterances confidently predicted
that the immediate and inevitable result of the Union
would be civil war. But this uncertainty of the ground
on which they stood had the natural effect of aggra-
vating men's passions and prompting them to devious
courses. Ignorant of the strength or weakness of
their opponents, the leaders of the different parties
at one time sought to better their position by compromise ; at another to crush their enemies by extreme
measures.

III

The conflicting aims of the different parties which
distracted the country will sufficiently appear in the
lectures that are to follow, but it is desirable that we
should have before us their respective positions at the
beginning of Anne's reign. It was by the force of
Presbyterianism that the Revolution of 1689 had been
effected in Scotland, and, but for its support, neither
William nor Anne could have maintained their rule
over that country. But even under William the
Presbyterians had not been wholly contented subjects.
Under him, indeed, Presbyterianism had been established as the national religion, but his toleration of
Episcopacy they could not understand, and for two
reasons : Episcopacy had not the sanction of Scripture,
and Episcopalians, as being reduced to the condition of
dissenters, were necessarily disloyal subjects. It was
with increased disquiet, however, that they regarded
the accession of Anne : ' sad things seem to be

threatened,'[1] wrote one of them in his Diary at the time. They were well aware of Anne's passionate attachment to the Church of England, and they knew from experience what pressure could be brought to bear on the Ministers who represented her in Scotland. Moreover, it was a deep-rooted suspicion of the Presbyterians that a Stewart must necessarily be a Papist at heart. Queen Mary had refused to adopt Protestantism when it was established as the religion of the country, and, though James VI and his two successors were nominally Protestants, they were all three in turn suspected of leanings towards Rome as the natural ally of rulers. In James VII they had seen all their suspicions justified : in openly avowing himself a Roman Catholic he had only logically carried out the uniform ecclesiastical policy of his immediate predecessors. His daughter Anne had refused to adopt the religion of her father, and might be sincerely attached to the Church of England, but from the beginning, in the eyes of Presbyterians, the Church of England was only a halfway house to Rome. It was in a permanent state of alternating hope and fear, therefore, that the Presbyterian body regarded the course of events throughout the whole of Anne's reign. They could not disabuse themselves of the conviction that it must be Anne's natural desire to restore Episcopacy in Scotland as a Church polity more in accordance with her conception of the royal prerogative than Presbyterianism, and they had the impression, shared by others besides themselves, that she was favourably disposed to the succession of her

---

[1] *Turnbull's Diary.*—Miscellany of the Scottish History Society, vol. i, p. 432.

brother James—a known Roman Catholic. For these various reasons the successive Ministries in Scotland found the Presbyterians a difficult body to conciliate. They were the mainstay of the new order established by the Revolution, but, as they could not get all they wanted, at more than one critical juncture their course of action was the occasion of serious alarm to those responsible for the conduct of affairs. Be it said, however, that there was one consideration that effectually kept their opposition within bounds : the only alternative for the Revolution settlement was a Roman Catholic king, and, in every probability, a Catholic State.

It is the main body of the Presbyterians that has just been before us, but there was a section of them who took up a more hostile attitude to the Government, and who were a serious element of opposition to be reckoned with. These were the men known as Cameronians (a designation, it should be said, somewhat loosely used in the documents of the time), who derived their name from Richard Cameron, the earliest of their most prominent leaders. They had taken shape as a definite body in the reign of Charles II, when, in their famous manifesto known as the 'Sanquhar Declaration', they had formally disowned Charles as their king on the ground of 'his perfidy and breach of covenant to God and his Kirk'. By this act they had dissociated themselves from the main body of their communion, whom they considered to have paltered with their consciences and to have been false to the principles of their common Presbyterianism. They joyfully hailed the Revolution as the promise of deliverance and of a reign in which a Covenanted king would rule over a Covenanted people. In their confident zeal they even formed a regiment to do battle against the fallen tyrant, and at Dunkeld, under the leadership of the gallant Colonel Clelland, they inflicted a defeat on a body of Highlanders which was more decisive for the course of events than the more famous battle of Killiecrankie. But William's reign had not well begun before they discovered how wofully they had deluded themselves. William, though he came from a country where Calvinism prevailed, no more than Charles and James was prepared to subscribe the Covenants, and, wakened to disillusion, they consistently refused to acknowledge either William or Anne as their lawful sovereign. Their own numbers would not have made them a very formidable body, but throughout the reign, as we shall see, they were by a strange contingency the objects of a vague terror to every successive Ministry.

Another irreconcilable body with whose hostility the Government had to reckon was the Episcopal clergy. In England the great majority of national churchmen had welcomed the Revolution, secure in the popular support that would leave William no choice but to continue the existing establishment. In Scotland the Episcopal Church had no such popular support behind it, and, from the very conditions under which William became King of Scotland, it seemed that he must become the necessary instrument of its doom. So far as circumstances would permit, William did his best to conciliate the Episcopalian section of his subjects, but no terms he was able to offer could make up for what they had lost, and to the end they regarded him as an unwelcome usurper who had sacrificed them to the

exigencies of his position. His successor Anne they
were bound to regard with more favour as being
a Stewart and stanchly devoted to the Church of
England. In the beginning of her reign they even
entertained some hope that, with her known religious
sympathies, supported too by English statesmen and
the whole strength of the Church of England, she
might find herself in a position that would enable her
to undo the work of William and restore them as the
national Church. The opening years of Anne's reign
were sufficient to undeceive them. Anne exerted all
her influence to better their condition, but from her
English and Scottish advisers alike she knew that any
attempt to upset the existing arrangement in Scotland
would be to imperil her rule in that country. To the
government of Anne, therefore, they were as hostile
as to that of William, and they were not careful to
conceal their feelings. On the occasion of the attempt
of 1708 to win Scotland for the exiled Prince they
openly expressed their hopes that the attempt might
succeed, though that Prince was as firm a Catholic as
his father.

The mention of the name Catholic reminds us of
another element in the country which was regarded
with a vague dread and concentrated hate, alike by
the mass of the people and by the majority of the
Scottish statesmen of the time. In England, as we
know, these feelings were not absent, and they had
been potent national motives at more than one period
of her history. But for special reasons they were in
intenser degree an obsession of the Scottish people.
The creed adopted by Scotland at the Reformation
went further in its divergence from the teaching of

Rome than that of any other form of Protestantism.
It was, moreover, only after a life-and-death struggle
that the new Church had succeeded in establishing
itself as the Church of the nation, and it had ever
since been haunted by the dread of a renewal of the
battle. The terror of Rome was the predominating
motive in the revolt against Charles I, and in the
evoking of the two Covenants. And this panic fear
was not confined to the Presbyterians: the Episcopalians were equally haunted by it. During the
Episcopalian ascendancy in the reign of Charles II,
penal laws against Catholics were enforced with as
great severity as at any period since the Reformation.
When James VII proposed to abolish these penal
laws, the clergy of the diocese of Aberdeen, the most
intensely Episcopalian part of the kingdom, laid
a protest before their bishop against the iniquity of
the proceeding. Even the Revolution did not allay
the fear of the common enemy. During the reigns of
William and Anne, no matter more frequently engaged the attention of the Scottish Privy Council than
the necessity of extirpating the dangerous brood who
were believed to be sleeplessly engaged in the attempt
to undermine the existing Church and State. The
conditions that obtained under Anne were such as
to make the presence of Catholics in the country
more dreaded than at any previous period. Among the
impelling forces by which the Union of 1707 was
eventually effected, the dread of Rome, so far as
Scotland was concerned, was not the least potent.
The Presbyterians shrank from the Union as likely
to result in the restoration of Episcopacy: but, as
their sagest leader, Carstares, warned them, there was

a more dread possibility if the Union did not take
place; they might find themselves one day at the
mercy of a Roman Catholic king.

IV

More or less closely associated with these three
religious denominations were three political parties
who made use of them as their own interests dictated.
These three parties were respectively known as the
Court Party, the Country Party, and the Jacobites or
Tories. The leaders of the Court Party were the
successive Ministries appointed by the sovereign for
the conduct of public affairs in Scotland. The duties
of the Ministers were to manage the business of the
Privy Council, and to carry out such measures in
Parliament as the advisers of the sovereign approved.
The appointment of the chief Officers of State had
been a matter of standing controversy between the
later Stewart kings and their Parliaments. Before
the reign of James VI, they had been appointed by the
sovereign with the advice of his Parliament, but
James VI assumed the power of appointing them by
his own fiat. In 1641 the Covenanting Parliament
had extorted from Charles I the concession that
thenceforth all Officers of State, Privy Councillors,
and Judges should be chosen by the sovereign 'with
the advice and approbation of the Estates'. At the
Restoration, Charles II reverted to the practice of his
father and grandfather, and appointed privy councillors and judges on his own responsibility. This
example was followed by James VII, and, what is
remarkable, it was also followed by William and Anne.

We see, then, how the designation 'Court Party' arose. The Privy Counc , which, besides the chief Ministers, included about fifty of the most influential men in the country, and the Judges of the Court of Session, with other legal officials, were all the nominees of the Crown and bound to do its bidding at the risk of losing their places. And, further, the Ministers of State bore gifts in their hands : they had it in their power to bestow pensions, to appoint to lucrative posts, and generally to distribute the sunshine of the Court. Thus the Court Party came to be regarded as the mere creatures of English Ministers, who dismissed them at their pleasure, and by the Country Party and the Jacobites alike they were suspected and opposed as the betrayers of their country.

In opposition to the Court Party, the Country Party put themselves forward as the champions of the national interests. Their contention was that, under the successive kings since the Union of the Crowns, the interests of Scotland had been systematically sacrificed to the interests of England. At the Revolution they saw the opportunity of righting the wrong, and, as the most effectual means to this end, they directed their efforts to the curtailing of the prerogative and enlarging the privileges of the Scottish Parliament. The disastrous enterprise of Darien, the failure of which the nation at large attributed to England, had the natural result of swelling their ranks and intensifying their patriotism. They became, indeed, what may be called the national party, though their main support came from the Presbyterians, who saw in their policy of freeing the Scottish Parliament from English control the most likely means of pre-

serving their Church. With this formidable party,
till the Union of 1707, the Ministers had to deal in
carrying through the measures with which they had
been entrusted by the Crown. The third political
party, the Jacobites—composed of Catholics and
Protestants—were few in numbers compared with the
Country Party, but the state of opinion, both inside
the Parliament and out of it, gave them an influence
out of proportion to their numbers. Their aim was
simply to discredit the government in the eyes of the
country and create such a general discontent that the
nation must at length realize that the Revolution had
been a disaster, and that the only hope for the future
was the return of the exiled Stewart. These aims
divided them by a gulf from the Country Party, who
had no desire to undo the work of the Revolution,
which at least had brought a measure of liberty
unknown under Charles II and James VII. But the
two parties had one common object—to embarrass
the Ministers by all the means in their power—and, in
point of fact, it was their alliance that, contrary to
their desires and intentions, was the direct occasion of
the Treaty of Union.

V

Such were the main divisions of opinion in politics
and religion which continued to exist even after the
Union, and which, indeed, did not cease to exist till
the failure of the Jacobite Rising of 1745. But besides
these divisions of parties there was a cleavage in the
kingdom itself which the statesmen of the time were
never allowed to forget. In the case of political
parties it is the Lowland country that we have mainly

in view. But there was another part of the country where little interest was taken in political divisions, but where the general tendency of events was followed with the closest interest. It was that Highland territory which, from the time that Scotland had become a united kingdom, had been a perennial source of trouble to her kings. In the reign of James VI a systematic and drastic policy had reduced these 'peccant parts', as they are described in the Acts of the Scottish Parliament, to comparative peace and order. Under Charles I there was a steady relapse into lawlessness, which was vigorously checked under the Commonwealth and Protectorate. During the reign of Charles II their condition was what it had been in the Middle Ages. It was the duty of his Scottish Privy Council to enforce the law throughout the length and breadth of the kingdom, but, so far as the Highlands were concerned, it was impotent to make the king's writ run. The Highlands were in this condition at the Revolution, and events in the reign of William were not such as to improve it. Hitherto they had shown no special affection for the Stewarts, for their rising under Montrose was due to other motives; and in every reign they had more or less successfully defied their authority. Then came the rising of certain of the clans under Dundee, and henceforward the Highlands became the seed-plot of Jacobite hopes. Throughout the reign of Anne all who were for the Protestant succession knew that the Highlands were a standing menace to their policy. They were the most warlike section of the people, and, in the event of civil war, which was imminent on at least one occasion during the reign, they would in all probability decide the issue in favour of the Stewart. Be it said that the government never had it in its power to assert its authority with the strong hand over the unruly territory. There were garrisons, indeed, in different parts of the country, and there were troops specially set apart for suppressing local revolt, but they were totally inadequate to overawe the clans in the event of a common rising. The most effectual means of holding them in check was, in truth, found to be a systematic pensioning of the chiefs—a policy that was followed throughout the reign.

A few words remain to be said on a point which is all-important for the understanding of Scotland's attitude towards England in the years immediately preceding the Union. Since the Union of the Crowns there had been a steadily growing conviction that the successive kings had treated Scotland as a mere appendage of their greater kingdom. In a notable sentence, written shortly after he received the English Crown, James VI describes his relations to the kingdom he had left. ' This I must say for Scotland,' he wrote, ' and may truly vaunt it : here I sit and govern it with my pen : I write and it is done ; and by a Clerk of the Council I govern Scotland now—which others could not do by the sword.' The policy of James was that of all the successors of his house. The Privy Council, composed of their nominees, was made the instrument of their will, and the Parliament, in the words of a loyalist historian of the time, became their ' baron court '. Thus no class in the country had the means of influencing policy either in its own interests or in the interests of the nation. Bereft of political liberty, the nation received no compensation in more favourable conditions of trade and commerce. The Navigation Act and the Act for the Encouragement of Trade, passed by the English Parliament in 1660 and 1663, permanently cut off the Scots from the principal sources of the world's wealth. Moreover, England's wars with Holland and France ruined their trade with their best customers. Nor was trade with England improved by the Union of the Crowns; on the contrary, the two countries came to be engaged in a war of tariffs in which the poorer of necessity came off worse. The feelings of resentment, roused by all these grievances, were not confined to one class or party; and it was with a jealous and embittered people that English statesmen had to deal in their endeavours to establish happier relations between the two kingdoms.

Such, in broad outline, was the political condition of Scotland at the accession of Anne, but even from the general statements that have been made it is evident that the reign would be fraught with the gravest possibilities. It was the opinion of all Scottish parties that the existing relations with England could not continue, and that the problem as to how the two countries should finally adjust their common interests must sooner or later have to be faced. It was a problem which, in the case of Scotland, was bound to evoke passions that might well threaten to rend her in twain. And, as was already said, there would be one factor in the new situation which would profoundly differentiate the reign of Anne from that of her predecessor. Under William both England and Scotland recognized Anne as his successor. But who was to succeed Anne remained to her death a disturbing question for both peoples. Would both agree to accept a common sovereign? In Scotland would Jacobite or Whig prove the stronger? By this uncertainty of eventualities the reign of Anne possesses something of the character of a drama—the final issue of which is awaited with anxious expectancy. And, if we choose to regard the reign in this light, we may apportionate it into three acts. The first act will cover the opening three years of the reign, which ended in the passing of the Act of Security—the immediate occasion of the Treaty of Union; the second, the two following years, during which the statesmen of both countries succeeded in carrying it into effect; and the third, the seven remaining years, during which it seemed that in the natural course of things the Union would have to be undone. Under these three divisions I propose to treat the events of the reign.

It was in view of this menacing state of the nation that the Council, as the custodian of the existing order, took the necessary steps to uphold it. Two regiments on the point of embarking for Holland were ordered to remain at home, and the commanders of the castles of Dumbarton and Stirling were instructed to see that these strongholds were in a state of efficient defence against attack. As the parts of the country where trouble was most likely to arise, special attention was given to the Highlands. The officer in command at Fort William, which had been constructed at the beginning of the late reign with the express object of overawing the West Highland country, was ordered to call in his subordinates, and to put the place 'in the best condition'. Since the reign of Charles II there had been two standing independent Highland companies expressly raised for the suppression of disorder, and the commanders of these companies were now ordered to hold themselves in readiness for active service.

On the day following, in expectation of further news regarding the king's condition, the Council held an extraordinary meeting, and during its afternoon *sederunt* an express messenger arrived with the news that the king had died four days previously. The messenger brought two other communications—one from the queen and the other from the Earl of Seafield, the Secretary of State for Scotland. The letter of Anne bore that all persons in public trust were meanwhile to retain their posts, and that of Seafield stated that the new sovereign had taken the coronation oath in the presence of ten Scottish Privy Councillors.

Its authority now sanctioned, the Council, in a suc-

LECTURE II

PROSPECTS OF UNION

I

On March 11, 1702, the Privy Council of Scotland sat in its usual place of meeting in Holyrood House. The *sederunt* must have been a gloomy one, as on the margin of his Minutes the Clerk of the Council has written these words—'extraordinary sad Council'.[1] The occasion of the Council's sadness was a letter from the Duke of Queensberry intimating 'the dangerous state of his Majesties life'. The prime function of the Privy Council was the maintenance of the public peace, and the orders it issued on Queensberry's communication sufficiently explain the grounds of its disquiet. During the closing years of William's reign, the country had been in a state of wild excitement, mainly occasioned by the disastrous result of the attempt to found a trading colony on the isthmus of Darien. In the Parliament, which had sat under Queensberry as Commissioner representing the king, there had been an unprecedented display of national feeling that was ominous for the future. 'God help us,' wrote one in June 1700, 'we are ripening for destruction.'[2]

---

[1] Minutes of Privy Council Register in the General Register House, Edinburgh (unpublished).

[2] W. Carstares, *State Papers*, ed. M'Cormick, Edin. 1774, p. 527.

cession of meetings, proceeded to issue such orders as were most urgently demanded by the condition of the country. As the measures it took bring home to us the permanent preoccupations of the government throughout the entire reign, it is necessary that we should have the most important of these measures before us. There were two main concerns that exercised the Council till its abolition in 1708, the year after the Union of the Parliaments of the two kingdoms, and which continued to exercise the government till the close of the reign. The one concern was the possibility of internal revolt in concert with foreign invasion; the other was the sinister presence of the emissaries of Rome, who in Highlands and Lowlands were unceasingly at work in the attempt to undermine the existing Church and State. Although the new sovereign had now been formally acknowledged by both kingdoms, it was still considered necessary to guard against a possible rising. The whole store of powder manufactured at a powder-mill near Edinburgh was appropriated by the government. The magistrates of every burgh in the country were ordered to seize all the powder within their respective bounds and to retain it till they received further orders. The two regiments which had been prohibited from embarking for Holland were still aboard the vessels which were to transport them, and the commander of the vessels was imprisoned till all the men were landed. Finally, measures were taken to ensure the efficiency of the two Highland companies, and a special commission was appointed to report on the growth of Popery throughout the Highlands and Western Islands.[1] These measures taken

[1] Minutes of the Privy Council.

by the Council will sufficiently indicate the conditions under which the reign of Anne began in Scotland, and they were conditions that continued to its close.

At this point, so far as the leading events of the reign are concerned, our interest in the Privy Council ceases. There had been a time, indeed, when it was the most important body in the country, the centre of interest in the national life. In the reigns of the later Stewarts it was the formidable instrument that gave effect to the fiats of the successive sovereigns. While the Parliament was reduced to a mere 'baron court', as the loyalist historian called it, and was summoned only at long intervals, the Council permanently sat, and, with the king's will behind it, laid down the law for 'all estates, persons, and causes whatsoever'. At the Revolution all this was changed. The Council continued to exist, and, as under the Stewarts, was composed of the king's nominees, but under the new constitution it was not in his power merely to indicate his pleasure to the Council with the certainty that it would be carried out with unquestioning submission. Consequently, throughout the reign of William we hear little of the Council, and are, indeed, hardly reminded of its existence. And so it was throughout the reign of his successor. Individual members of it, as holding government office, were among the leading actors of the time, but, as a corporate body, it may be ignored. So far as its relation to the current of events is concerned, we have only to note that, as charged with the maintenance of the public order, it had occasionally to exercise its powers in restraining the Edinburgh mob when it broke beyond bounds.

II

It was another body to which the eyes of the nation were now turned—to the Parliament which was no longer the 'baron court' it had been under Charles II and his brother. As a consequence of the Revolution, the Scottish Parliament assumed new characteristics, and, as has often been pointed out, it began to emulate the ways and methods of the Parliament of England. Notably, in the second year of William's reign, it succeeded in gaining an advantage after which it had long striven : it obtained his consent to the abolition of the Committee known as the Lords of the Articles. Under the later Stewarts the grievance against these Lords had been that, as the creatures of the Court, and with the powers at their disposal, they were virtually the dictators of the Estates. With the abolition of the Committee of the Articles, the Parliament acquired the power of free debate on every Bill before the House. Yet, as was keenly felt, it was still far from being a legislative body with powers to give effect to the national will. The Commissioner who presided over its meetings was appointed by the Crown, and he came down from London with definite commands regarding the measures to which he was to give or refuse the royal sanction. By his side were the other Ministers of State, who held their offices on the condition that they gave their support to the Commissioner in carrying out his instructions. Thus, so far as practical legislation was concerned, Parliament was still an ineffectual body. But, as was convincingly shown during the last years of William, it had weapons in its hands which it could use with effect. It could obstruct the royal measures by endless debate; and by delaying supply it could, on occasion, so embarrass the government as to extract its own terms. Such as it was, therefore, the Scottish Parliament was now, what it had never been previous to the Revolution, a real force in the State, and sovereign and people alike recognized the fact. Till the close of its last session, which ended with the Treaty of Union, the doings of the Parliament were the all-absorbing interest of the country, as it was realized that the destinies of the nation were in its hands.

To the meeting of the Parliament, therefore, all parties looked forward with anxious expectancy as likely to be decisive of their fortunes in the new reign. And there were special reasons to anticipate that its meeting would be signalized by a testing trial of strength which would definitely determine into what hands the future administration of the country was to fall. The Parliament that was about to meet was the Convention which, at the Revolution, had offered the Crown to William and Mary. On the accession of the new sovereigns the Convention had been erected into a Parliament which, to the growing dissatisfaction of the country, had continued to sit to the close of William's reign. The grievance was that it no longer represented the opinion of the country, and that it was contrary to the constitution that so long a period should elapse without a general election. This would be one ground of contention when it met at the beginning of the new reign. But a more serious question arose before its actual meeting. By an Act of the late reign (1696), similar to one passed by the Parliament of

England, it had been settled that the existing Parliament should meet twenty days after the king's death, should not sit for longer than six months, and that its powers should be restricted to measures for the conservation of Church and State.

The Parliament did not meet within the prescribed twenty days, and the fact gave to its discontented members an opportunity which was not to be let slip. If it were now an illegal body, a new election was a necessity. This was the point that was now pressed home by the leaders of the various parties who were at one in their determination to force an appeal to the country. The leader of these parties for the time was one who by his rank, his influence, and his gifts was the most notable figure among the Scottish statesmen of the reign—James, fourth Duke of Hamilton. He was a prince of the blood, and, failing direct heirs to the House of Stewart, he had the nearest claim to the Crown. Since the beginning of the reign of Mary Stewart every one of his ancestors had been suspected of playing his own game with a view to the throne, and the same suspicion attached to himself. So dubious had been his past career and so dubious was it to be in the future, that his friends and his enemies were equally at a loss to understand the motives of his conduct. He had been chosen President of the Convention that offered the Crown to William, and William had made him Royal Commissioner when the Convention was turned into a Parliament. He was twice imprisoned in the Tower on the suspicion of plotting for the restoration of the exiled king, yet he had consented to receive honours and titles from William's hands. It was he who, in the last years of William,

had led the opposition in Parliament, and, even by the
admission of his enemies, had shown many of the most
effective gifts of an opposition leader. He is described
by a contemporary as of 'middle stature, well-made, of
a black, coarse complexion, a brisk look';[1] and an
English visitor to Edinburgh who heard him in the
House speaks of his 'usual haughty and bantering
air'.[2] To his effectiveness in debate there is consenting
testimony; though not eloquent, says Lockhart, 'he
had so nervous, majestick, and pathetick a method of
speaking, and applying what he spoke, that it was
always valued and regarded'.[3] Along with these gifts,
however, he had grave defects which unfitted him to be
the trusted leader of a party. According to Lockhart,
who was not disposed to say the worst of him, 'his
greatest failing lay in his being too selfish and revenge-
ful, which he carried along with him in all his designs
. . .' An attractive figure he certainly is not, whether
judged by his words or his deeds, yet when Lockhart,
summing up his character, concludes that he was 'a
great and extraordinary man', he expressed the opinion
of his friends and enemies alike. As the documents
of the time show, what the Duke of Hamilton would
say or do was the subject of anxious concern to men
of all shades of opinion.

The day prescribed for the meeting of Parliament
having passed, Hamilton and others of the political
leaders proceeded to London to present their case to the
queen and her English Ministers. The English Parlia-

---

[1] *Memoirs of the Secret Services of John Macky, Esq.*, Lond., 1733
pp. 176–8.

[2] *A Journey to Edenborough*, pp 111–2.

[3] *The Lockhart Papers*, Lond., 1817, vol. i, p. 55.

ment had been summoned three days after William's death ; that the Scottish Parliament had not been summoned with a similar promptness seemed to indicate hesitations on the part of Anne's advisers. In point of fact, they had consulted the Scottish Council, which had given the opinion that there was no necessity that the Parliament should meet before the expiry of the twenty days.[1] When Hamilton and his friends arrived in London, therefore, they were given to understand not only that the Parliament would meet in due course, but that it would meet as a legal assembly, and that the Ministry which had been in power under William would remain virtually the same. Only one course was now left open to them : they would do their best in the House itself to make business impossible.

The Parliament met at length on June 9, and, as a pledge to the country that there was to be no immediate change in policy, the Duke of Queensberry was continued in the office of Royal Commissioner which he had held under William. After the Duke of Hamilton Queensberry is the most outstanding of the Scottish political leaders of the time. As in the case of Hamilton, his complex character made him something of a mystery to his contemporaries, though no two men could present a greater contrast. Hamilton was violent, headstrong, overbearing; Queensberry was all suavity and plausibility, though behind his soft demeanour he concealed a tenacity of purpose which was to be signally shown in the career that still lay before him. 'His Grace', says one who knew him well, 'was a compleat courtier, and partly by art, and partly by nature, he had brought himself into a habite

[1] Hume of Crossrig, *Diary*, Ban. Club, 1827, pp. 80–1.

of saying very oblidging things to everybody. I knew
his character, and therefore was not much elated by
his promises. However, I found afterwards that there
was nothing he had promised to do for me but what
he made good.'[1] He was now in his fiftieth year,
experienced in public business, and the most prominent
representative in Scotland of Revolution principles.
He had been the first Scotsman, says the Jacobite
Lockhart, 'that deserted over to the Prince of Orange,
and from thence acquired the epithet (amongst honest
men) of "Proto-rebel".'[2] Be it added that Queensberry
and Hamilton were already bitter enemies, not only
by reason of political differences, but of personal and
family rivalry.[3]

The question naturally suggests itself: Why did the
Tory advisers who surrounded Anne at the beginning
of her reign consent to the continuance of a Scottish
Parliament in which the majority was Whig, and
a Ministry which was exclusively Whig? The truth
is that they had no sure information regarding the
state of public opinion in Scotland. It was the habit
of the English Ministers who had charge of Scottish
affairs to hold secret communications with the representatives of all parties, and the advice they received
was so conflicting that they found it impossible to
follow out a settled policy. What might be the result

[1] Sir John Clerk, *Memoirs*, Scot. Hist. Soc., 1892, p. 44.

[2] *Memoirs*, i, p. 44.

[3] The second Earl of Stair wrote as follows to the Earl of Mar on
Queensberry's death: 'I am touched to the quick for losing our very
good friend the Duke of Queensberry, who was the best natured,
friendly man I ever knew. He had some very great qualities and
many very good ones; his defects hurt only himself.'—*Duke of
Portland's MSS.*, Hist. MSS. Com., vol. v, p. 43.

of a general election at the moment was uncertain, and meantime they had to face a practical difficulty. The Scottish treasury was empty, and money was needed to pay the troops which the state of feeling in the country made indispensable. With a reasonable amount of confidence they could reckon on the existing Parliament and Ministry finding supply ; but they could have no such confidence in the case of a new Parliament. For the time, therefore, they thought it advisable to leave things as they had stood at the death of William.

In order to follow the proceedings of the Parliament now about to meet it is desirable that we should have some idea of its place of meeting, and of its character as a legislative assembly, so essentially different from that of the Parliament of England. From the beginning the three Scottish Estates, like those in France, had sat in one chamber. In earlier times they had met indifferently in any of the more important burghs, though from the beginning of the sixteenth century Edinburgh was their usual place of assembly. Till 1641 they had no chamber specially set apart for them even in Edinburgh, but in 1631 Charles I informed the magistrates that, if they did not construct a fitting place for their accommodation, they would cease to meet in the capital. Under this threat the magistrates carried out the building of an edifice which should include accommodation both for the Law Courts and for the Parliament. It was in the noble hall then constructed—the same now industriously trodden by advocates awaiting the call of anxious litigants [1]—that

---

[1] The hall has undergone certain structural changes since the Parliament met in it.

the Parliament of Scotland now held its deliberations. On the south side of the Hall was the Commissioner's throne, where he sat in silence through the prolonged debates, with the silken purse containing his commission on the cushion before him. Beneath him sat the Lord Chancellor, the President of the House; on his right the Lord Treasurer, and on his left the chief Secretary of State. At one end of the long table that occupied the body of the Hall, and on which were disposed the Crown, Sceptre, and Sword (the 'Honours' of Scotland), was the Lord Justice-Clerk; at the other, the Lord Marischal. To the right and left of the Commissioner the benches rose in tiers, on which the members were arranged in accordance with their rank. On the uppermost seats to the right were the dukes, marquesses, and earls, and under them the representatives of the shires; and on those to the left, the viscounts and barons, and beneath them the representatives of the burghs. At the opposite end of the Hall, facing the throne, but outside the area, was the pulpit from which sermons were occasionally delivered during the course of the session; and behind the pulpit was a partition, beyond which strangers were not permitted to enter while the House was sitting. At the opening of each day's business prayers were said; then the rolls were called, and the Chancellor announced the question demanding the attention of the House. Members might speak only once to the matter in hand, and only when they were expressly called upon by the Chancellor. When a vote was taken, each member was asked if he approved or disapproved of the motion before the House. Such were the regulations for the conduct of business, but in the excited debates of the post-revolution Parliaments, they were constantly set at naught by the more impetuous members of all parties; and in the long evening sittings, when the Hall was dimly lit by the sporadic candles, there were frequent scenes of uproar and violence in which all restraint and decorum were thrown to the winds.

Till the beginning of the eighteenth century the number of members who sat in Parliament was under two hundred; in the Parliament that carried the Treaty of Union it amounted to two hundred and thirty-two, the largest number on record. As the clergy had been excluded at the Revolution, the membership consisted of three classes—the nobles, the Commissioners for the Shires, and the Commissioners for the Burghs. The nobles sat in virtue of their holding their lands direct from the Crown; in the case of the other two classes there was a form of election. At the period with which we are dealing, the privilege of electing Commissioners for the Shires was restricted to Crown vassals, not nobles, who held lands of the value of 40s. Each of the Royal Burghs, in number sixty-six, had a right to one representative; Edinburgh alone returned two. The electing bodies were the town councils of the burghs, and for the whole country did not exceed 2,000. We see, therefore, how inadequately the two elected Estates represented national opinion. And the smallness of the electorate had its natural results. The freeholders who elected the Commissioners for the Shires, being so few in number, were easily accessible to the blandishments of the existing government, and by the bestowal of pensions and offices they could be induced to return acceptable representatives.

F

And the case was worse with the town councils that
elected the Commissioners for the Burghs. By an
arrangement copied from France in the fifteenth
century the retiring town council elected its successor, so that it was virtually a stereotyped body,
at all times practically under the control of the Privy
Council as representing the sovereign from whom the
royal burghs held their privileges. Thus, in the case
both of the Commissioners for the Shires and the Commissioners for the Burghs, we have no certain assurance
that they represented the opinions of the majority of
the people. In the session of the Parliament with
which we are now concerned the representatives of
the Three Estates were approximately equal in
numbers; there were thirty-five nobles, thirty-eight
Commissioners of the Shires, and forty-three Commissioners of the Burghs. But these numbers by no
means represent the relative influence of each Estate
in the House. For evident reasons the nobles domi-
nated the assembly to an extent out of all proportion
to their relative numbers. At a time when feudal
feeling was still powerful, their rank and possessions
gave them an ascendancy over both the minor barons
and the burghers which was also due to the great part
they had played in the past history of the country.
But for the nobility the Reformation could not have
been effected; it was they who made possible the
great revolt against Charles I; it was they who were
mainly instrumental in restoring Charles II in Scotland;
and it was owing to them more than to the other two
Estates that the Treaty of Union was eventually
carried. Be it added that the chief offices of state
were in their hands; that, as a body, they were in

closer touch with the higher powers in London; and that there were among them at this time men with notable gifts for public business and for Parliamentary debate.

The session opened with a dramatic incident for which the House was no doubt fully prepared. On prayers being said, the Duke of Hamilton rose and craved to be heard, when the Earl of Marchmont, the Lord Chancellor, reminded him that the House was not yet constituted. Hamilton replied that the right of that assembly to constitute itself a legal Parliament was precisely the point to which he wished to speak, and he proceeded to read a paper containing the protest of himself and his supporters. It briefly stated the grounds on which the protest was made : by the constitution of the kingdom, when a Parliament met at the sovereign's decease, its sole business was to secure the Protestant religion and to maintain the succession in accordance with the Claim of Right. Both of these ends were satisfied by the accession of the new sovereign, and, therefore, there was no legal warrant for the existence of the present assembly. Thereupon Hamilton, without handing in the paper, in Scottish phrase, 'took instruments', that is, legal attestation to his action, and walked out of the House at the head of fifty-seven members.[1] The public had apparently been prepared for the event, as a cheering crowd received the seceders, who marched in a body to a tavern in the neighbourhood, where they dined together, in Lockhart's words, 'to knit the public by the ties of private union'.[2]

[1] The number of the seceders is variously given.

[2] Lockhart, *Memoirs*, i. 45 ; *Acts of Parl. of Scot.*, xi, App., p. 1 ; Hume of Crossrig, *Diary*, p. 83.

Though Hamilton and his allies had retired from the House, they had not therefore given up the contest. They were still convinced that in her heart the queen could not regard with favour an assembly so entirely Whig and Presbyterian as the existing Scottish Parliament, and they knew that certain of her English advisers, like the Secretary of State, the Earl of Nottingham, were desirous of a new election. An unpublished correspondence of Hamilton informs us of the means employed by himself and his supporters to effect their end, and is further interesting as showing the extent to which Scottish affairs were dependent on England. An address, subscribed by Hamilton and others, was put in the hands of Lord Blantyre and a Mr. Keith, who were instructed to present it to the queen in her drawing-room. No one was to have a sight of the address till the queen herself had read it. Meanwhile Hamilton entered into communication with Anne's all-powerful favourite, Lady Marlborough, with the object of enlisting her support. Whether Lady Marlborough, who was a keen Whig, approached Anne on the subject or not, the correspondence does not inform us. Anne, at all events, to the surprise and chagrin of Hamilton, peremptorily refused to receive the address, and the proceedings of the Parliament, now in session, are a sufficient explanation of her refusal.[1] By the date when she rejected the address she had every reason to believe that the measures entrusted to her Commissioner Queensberry would receive the sanction of the House.

---

[1] *State Papers* (*Scotland*), Series II, vol. i, nos. 12, 13, 14, 15, Record Office.

Connected with Hamilton's protest is an incident so nationally characteristic that it can hardly be passed over. The Faculty of Advocates was one of the most important public bodies in the country, representing, as it did, the law of the kingdom, and claiming to have received the royal sanction so far back as 1532, the date of the foundation of the College of Justice. The advocates, one hundred and forty-five in number, were all men of high social position, the sons of nobles or lairds, and were thus both personally and professionally persons of influence. As a body, they were keenly Tory in their sympathies. To the indignation of the sitting Whig Parliament it came to its knowledge that the Dean of the Faculty had drafted an address to the queen in support of the seceding members, and that the address had been signed by a number of the advocates. The Dean and his professional brethren were promptly summoned to the bar of the House to give an explanation of their conduct. Seventy declared that they had had no hand in the business, but twenty 'young men of no note' refused to answer the questions put to them. The House was unanimous that the advocates in drafting such an address had gone beyond their powers as a corporation, but it was divided as to the degree of their guilt. Some held that they had been guilty of a 'misdemeanour', others that their conduct was 'unwarrantable', and others still that the address was 'a high insult against the Queen and Parliament'. Eventually the offenders were handed over to the Privy Council as the special body appointed to deal with crimes against the State. The sager heads in the House, however, were of opinion that it would have been more prudent to take no notice of the address which, as in the case of that of the seceders, the queen would have refused to receive.

III

After the secession of Hamilton and his followers the remaining members were, according to Lockhart, 'all one man's bairns', and they proceeded to act as a legally constituted Parliament. They passed an act recognizing her Majesty's authority, and another which declared the present assembly of Parliament to be a lawful meeting. On the third day of the session there occurred a scene which deserves a passing notice, not only as revealing the temper of the House itself, but as indicative of the popular feeling which had to be reckoned with in all the dealings of the English Ministers with Scotland. It was this popular feeling, as we shall see, that was to prove the greatest obstacle to the Treaty of Union, as indeed it marked the deepest cleavage between the past and the present of the two countries. There had just been read an act for securing the true Protestant religion and Presbyterian government, when the Commissioner for the burgh of Sanquhar, Sir Alexander Bruce of Broomhall, rose to address the House. A distinction, he said, had to be made between the Protestant religion and Presbyterian Church government, for it might easily be proved that Presbyterianism as now established was essentially inconsistent with monarchy. Instantly there was a cry from all parts of the House : ' To the Bar, to the Bar.' Two speakers suggested that, though Bruce deserved censure, he should be allowed either to explain himself or ask pardon of the House, but the cry was again raised : 'To the Bar.' Proceeding to the Bar, Bruce pleaded that he had meant to say only that he *conceived* Presbyterianism to be inconsistent with monarchy. The explanation was considered unsatisfactory, and he was ordered to leave the House, when it was put to the vote whether he should be expelled from the House or not. Without a dissentient voice his expulsion was voted, and the order was issued for a new Commissioner for Sanquhar. But even this punishment was regarded as inadequate for the enormity of his offence, and the Privy Council, as the guardian of the peace, was instructed to deal with him. Summoned to its bar, he failed to appear, when, as was the law in such a case, he was 'put to the horn', and his speech ordered to be burned at the Town Cross of Edinburgh by the common hangman.[1] The whole incident proves that, so far as Presbyterianism was concerned, the 'Rump', as the mutilated assembly was contemptuously designated, were all 'one man's bairns'.

That they were not of one mind on all questions, however, was emphatically shown before the session closed. The question on which differences arose was one that deeply concerned the future relations of the two peoples. Immediately after Anne's accession the English Parliament had passed an act making it obligatory for all persons holding office to abjure her brother, the Pretender. A similar act for Scotland was passionately desired by the extreme Presbyterians, for whom the possibility of a Roman Catholic successor to the throne was a nightmare. The Commissioner Queensberry, as well as others of his colleagues, was

[1] Hume of Crossrig, *Diary*, pp. 88-9; Minutes of the Privy Council, July 28, Nov. 17, 1702.

in favour of passing such an act, and is even said to have received instructions to give it the royal assent.[1] The wariest of politicians, however, he was convinced that to propose such a measure would arouse passions which it would be prudent to let slumber. Not so circumspect, or more confident of the result, was his colleague, the Earl of Marchmont, the Lord Chancellor and President of the House. Marchmont, better known to his countrymen as Sir Patrick Hume, was, till the passing of the Treaty of Union, among the most prominent of the Scottish political leaders. None of them certainly had had a more eventful career. Under Charles II he had been imprisoned for his opposition to the policy of Lauderdale. He was charged with being accessory to the Rye-house Plot, and it is one of the best known stories in Scottish history how he lay concealed in the vault of Polwarth Church for a month and was kept alive by provisions secretly carried to him by his daughter. Escaping to Holland, he identified himself with the Prince of Orange, whose accession to the throne opened up to him a distinguished political career. Appointed Chancellor by William in 1696, he had been continued in the office by Anne. He is described as 'a fine gentleman', 'handsome and lovely', and much addicted to long speeches, even in private. As his career had shown, he was a Whig of the Whigs and a devotee of Presbytery.

It was to Queensberry's surprise and against his will that Marchmont introduced his bill for abjuring the Prince of Wales. Marchmont's reasons for insisting upon it were mainly two: it was necessary for securing the Revolution settlement, and it would exclude all

[1] Carstares, *State Papers*, pp. 71-4.

Jacobites and Papists from the next Parliament. On the first reading of the bill it was at once apparent how hopelessly the House was divided on the question : fifty-seven voted for a second reading, and fifty-three against it. As the result of the vote, party passions were let loose, and there was talk of the return of the members who had seceded to support the opponents of the bill. But in the interval Queensberry decided on his course of action ; on the day fixed for the second reading (June 30), he rose and quietly told the House that it was prorogued till the 18th of August following. In his suavest tones he referred to the dissensions that had arisen. ' I must regret,' he said, ' that, when I was expecting we should have parted in the same happy manner, a proposal, which I had some ground to think was laid aside, was offered to my surprise as well as that of her Majesty's other Ministers, which occasioned some debate and difference in the House.'[1]

Lockhart expresses his surprise that in an assembly comprised almost exclusively of Whig Presbyterians an act abjuring the Pretender should not have been passed without difficulty. But another contemporary gives the sufficient reason. There were two classes of Presbyterians among the members. There were those whose sole concern was the maintenance of the Presbyterian establishment ; and there were those who, while preferring Presbytery as a form of Church government, held it of greater moment to free their country from its dependence on England.[2] The reasons which

---

[1] Ib., pp. 714–7 ; *Marchmont Papers*, Lond., 1831, iii. 242–52 ; *Acts Parl. Scot.*, xi. 28.

[2] *Memorial by Lord Tarbat*, Add. MSS. Brit. Mus. 29587, f. 151.

induced these political Presbyterians to oppose the exclusion of the Pretender, therefore, are easily understood. By leaving the succession unsettled, England was made uneasy, and in her own interests might be forced to make concessions to her weaker neighbour. In the words of one who wrote at the time, the passing of Marchmont's bill 'would carry us so far into the measures of England about the succession that they would become careless and indifferent about the union.'[1]

The refusal of the Scottish Estates to pass an Act of Abjuration was a defiance to England; by the passing of another act with their full concurrence they held out the olive branch. It had been a dying request of William III that, in the interest of both kingdoms, an incorporating union should be consummated at the earliest possible date; had he lived, it was his intention to press the great question at the next meeting of the English Parliament. As was proved by her subsequent conduct, Anne was herself personally convinced of the desirability of union; and it was a proof of her conviction that her first act with reference to Scotland was to recommend it. In accordance with a suggestion made in her first speech to the English Parliament, a bill was passed ordaining that Commissioners of Union should be chosen from both countries, and it was a prime charge to Queensberry that he should secure a similar act from the Parliament of Scotland. From a body composed, as it was, almost exclusively of Whigs Queensberry had no difficulty in obtaining the required measure. By the terms of this act the queen was empowered to

---

[1] Carstares, *State Papers*, p. 715.

appoint Commissioners from both kingdoms, but it was expressly stipulated that the acceptance of their conclusions should be 'wholly reserved' for the Parliaments of the two kingdoms. Moreover, in a collective letter to Anne, intimating the passing of the act, she was given to understand that her Parliament in Scotland had sanctioned the appointment of Commissioners only on the condition that the Church, as established at the Revolution, should remain untouched.

Parliament prorogued, Queensberry hastened to London to give an account of his stewardship. On the whole he had discharged it successfully. He had at least contrived to secure the passing of two acts to which the queen and her English Ministers attached special importance. He had obtained sufficient supplies to support the Forces in Scotland for the next two years, and by securing the appointment of Commissioners of Union he had opened a way which might lead to happier relations between the two kingdoms. Yet no one knew better than himself what difficulties would have to be overcome before the consummation. The secession of Hamilton and his following, the strife that had arisen over the proposal to abjure the Pretender, were ominous indications of future party conflicts of which no one could foresee the result. All men now saw what fateful issues lay before the country in the reign that had opened, and they fully realized that a repetition of the Douglas Wars, when Scotland was desolated by internecine strife, was a frightful possibility.

A word in conclusion may be said regarding the proceedings of the Commission for Union. On the

10th of November, 1702, the Commissioners, twenty-
three for England and twenty-one for Scotland, met
in the Cockpit at Whitehall, then the Privy Council
chamber. The history of their proceedings proves
that on the part of England, at least, there was no
great eagerness for a successful issue. To the annoy-
ance of the Scots the English Commissioners gave
but irregular attendance, on eight occasions even
failing to make a quorum. It was of good omen,
however, that on two all-important points both bodies
were unanimous—that there should be a common
legislature and that, in accordance with the Act of
Settlement, the succession should descend on the
Electress Sophia and her heirs. But it was when
questions of trade and taxation came to be considered
that what were supposed to be the conflicting interests
of the two countries became clearly apparent. As
these difficulties had again to be faced at a later day,
they need not now detain us. What this abortive
Commission proved was that in neither country was
opinion sufficiently matured to exercise a compelling
force on its representatives. In the case of both
countries the experience of the next few years was
needed to supply the momentum requisite to overcome difficulties which now appeared insuperable.
When the Commission rose on February 3, 1703, it
was on the understanding that it should resume its
meetings in the following October; that it never
again met is a sufficient proof of its futility.

LECTURE III

THE ACT OF SECURITY

I

The Commissioner Queensberry, as we saw, after adjourning the Estates on the last day of June, 1702, at once proceeded to London. As it happened, England was now on the eve of a decisive change in the relative positions of her two political parties. On July 2, two days after the adjournment of the Scottish Estates, the Whig Parliament of William, which had continued to sit under Anne, was dissolved; and a general election followed, with the result that Tories were returned in the proportion of two to one. The ascendancy of the Tories in the new English Parliament necessarily influenced the policy of English Ministers towards Scotland, and this influence is clearly visible in Scottish affairs till another election three years later reversed the relative positions of the two parties. An unpublished letter of Speaker Harley to the Lord Treasurer Godolphin, dated August 9, already indicates a new departure in the administration of Scottish business.[1] The letter, it may be said, is interesting for other reasons. It shows Harley already manifesting that concern for eventualities in Scotland which continued to the close of the reign, and it indicates the tactics persistently followed by English Ministers in

[1] *Letters of Robert Harley*, Brit. Mus. Add. MSS. 28055, f. 3.

their dealings with the leaders of the various Scottish parties.

From Harley's letter we learn that Queensberry, while in London, had strongly expressed his opinion against the immediate election of a new Scottish Parliament. There was no urgent necessity for summoning it, Queensberry urged, as the late Parliament had voted supplies sufficient for the maintenance of the Forces till 1704. It was impossible to predict what would be the result of a general election at that time, and it was desirable that they should proceed cautiously. In the following November the constitution required that there should be an election of Commissioners of the Shires, though not for the burghs. If the result of that election should be encouraging, a general election might then be risked; if not, the election could be postponed till 1704, by which date the nation might be in a calmer state of mind.

The two English Ministers specially concerned with Scotland were Godolphin and the Secretary of State, the Earl of Nottingham. By the advice of both Queensberry's suggestion was rejected; the existing Parliament was dissolved, and the election of a new one fixed for the close of the year. This decision, be it said, may mark a turning-point in the history of both kingdoms. The Parliament that was actually elected was the last national assembly which Scotland was to elect, and it was the Parliament that was to pass the Treaty of Union. Had Queensberry's advice been followed, it is not improbable that so different a body might have been returned that other lights might have guided it and the Treaty have had far different fortunes. In 1704, the date which Queensberry proposed for the new election, other questions distracted the country, and the nation might have seen possibilities in the future which it did not see in 1702 and 1703.

The decision of the English Ministers for an immediate election was not well received by Queensberry and the majority that had supported him in the late Parliament. In the same letter of Harley we are told how the news was received by the different Scottish parties. There was to be a new Parliament, it was said, not because the nation desired it, but because such was the wish of the Earl of Nottingham. On the other hand, some raised the cry that it was out of deference to the Duke of Hamilton and the other seceders that the English Tories had consented to an immediate election. But the party most dismayed by the news was that section of the Presbyterian Whigs who put the Kirk before every other consideration, and, as we shall see, they had some grounds for their disquiet.

There were cogent reasons for the ferment into which the nation was thrown by the prospect of a general election. Under William there had been five general elections in England, whereas in Scotland the Convention that had been returned at the Revolution sat through the whole reign. It was after a space of fourteen years, therefore, that the nation had to choose a new body of representatives, so that the novelty of the occasion was in itself exciting. But there were grave reasons why this particular election should move the nation deeply. The Parliament elected would have to deal with issues which involved the very existence of the State. At the death of Anne was Scotland to have the same successor as England?

Was there or was there not to be a Treaty of Union between the two kingdoms? These questions the new Parliament would have to settle, and on the settlement effected the future of the nation must depend. And for many there was an even more anxious consideration. How would the Presbyterian form of Church government established at the Revolution fare at the hands of the new assembly?[1] A bill just passed by a great majority in the House of Commons was not fitted to allay the fears of these persons. It was the bill against Occasional Conformity, the object of which was to disqualify Dissenters from holding any public office. But, in the eyes of those who were responsible for that bill, all members of the Church of Scotland were dissenters. Would an English Tory Ministry not consider it at once a duty and its wisest policy to put Episcopacy in place of Presbytery as more consonant with the royal prerogative? It was with this possibility before them that the Presbyterian party put forth all their efforts to secure a safe majority in the new Parliament, and they had a powerful engine at their command. Throughout the country the pulpit was the potent agency to stir the people to action, and now, as at a later stage, the clergy were the efficient agents in promoting the interests of the party on whose support they depended for the preservation of their Church.

It is in connexion with the return of the new Parliament that another Scottish statesman of the reign comes decisively before us. This was James, Earl of

[1] On January 29, 1703, the Earl of Mar wrote to his brother: 'Presbytery is to be ruined.' This was, at least, the dread of the national clergy.

Seafield, who had been appointed joint-Secretary of State with Queensberry at the accession of Anne—an office which he had held during the last six years of William's reign. It was Seafield's distinction to be equally detested by the Jacobites and the Country or Patriotic Party. For the Jacobites he was a perjured traitor to their cause, and, at the same time, its most formidable enemy. He had given staunch support to James VII while he was yet king, and at the Revolution he had been one of five members of the Convention who entered their dissent against the act that declared James to have forfeited the crown. Subsequently he took the oaths to William and Mary, and served them as faithfully as he had served James. It will be seen, therefore, why the Jacobites regarded him with mingled hate and scorn. And in the eyes of the Country Party he was equally a traitor. In his official capacity under William he had dared to discountenance the Darien Scheme, with the result that for the mass of his countrymen he became the byword for a renegade Scot. So he was judged by his contemporaries whose aims he had thwarted. As it happens, however, we have ample materials from his own hand for forming an independent opinion of him, since his correspondence that has been preserved is more voluminous than that of any other Scottish politician of the time.[1] The impression we receive from his correspondence is that, unlike many of his contemporaries,

---

[1] His published correspondence will be found in the *Seafield Papers*, Hist. MSS. Com., Fourteenth Report, App. Part III, and in the *Seafield Correspondence*, Scot. Hist. Soc., vol. iii, second series. There is also a large collection of Seafield's letters in the Brit. Mus. Add. MSS. 28055, of which use is here made.

he had no political theories and that he belonged to the race of politicians who, in Dryden's words, 'neither love nor hate.' With such a mind and temper it seemed to him the best wisdom to support the powers that were, and to make himself an indispensable public servant. His constant refrain in his letters to English Ministers is that he considers it his sole business to give effect to their policy in the way that seems best to him. And Anne and her Ministers were convinced that they could not have a more efficient instrument. His friends and foes alike bear testimony to his tact and his capacity. 'He was finely accomplished,' says Lockhart, for whom he was the embodiment of every evil political principle; 'a learned lawyer, a just judge : courteous and good-natured;'[1] and another contemporary describes him as 'very beautiful in his person, with a graceful behaviour, a smiling countenance, and a soft tongue. . . .'[2]

It was this useful servant who was sent down by Anne and her Ministers to influence the elections in favour of their policy. The nature of the influence at his command has already been suggested. Some were threatened with the queen's displeasure ; to some were given pensions ; to others, offices ; to others still, promises of future rewards on condition of acceptable service. But with all his efforts Seafield failed to secure such a majority as would avert dangerous opposition to the measures of the Court. When on May 6, 1703, the new Parliament met, it was found to be somewhat differently composed from its predecessor. In that Parliament there had been two main parties :

[1] Lockhart, *Memoirs*, i. 52.   [2] Macky, *Memoirs*, p. 182.

the party that generally supported the measures of the government, and the Country Party, led by Hamilton, which generally opposed them. In the new Parliament there appeared a third party variously designated the Episcopal, the Cavalier, or the Jacobite party. As it was out of the conflict of these three parties that the union of the two kingdoms eventually resulted, it is desirable that we should have before us the respective objects for which they contended. The strictly Ministerial party, in each successive session, was committed to the support of such measures as were dictated by the English Ministers who chanced to be in power. To the last hour of the new Parliament's existence this party was in a minority, and it was only with the support of one or other of the opposing sections of the House that it was enabled to give effect to the royal instructions. The second party, the Presbyterians—described as 'the most numerous and the most eager party' in the House—were passionately bent on two objects—the maintenance of the Revolution Settlement as securing the Protestant religion, and the permanence of Presbytery as the established form of Church government. In the session about to begin it was fully realized by the Ministry that without the support of the Presbyterians no government measures had a chance of being carried. Finally, there was the Jacobite party, which, like the Presbyterians, had two ends that inspired all their action—the restoration of the exiled Stewart, and, as a consequence, the re-establishment of Episcopacy.[1] As a small minority in the House, the Jacobites could play only one game;

[1] Some of the Jacobites were Roman Catholics.

by fomenting discontent in the other two parties they could embarrass successive Ministries, discredit them in the eyes of the country, and so prepare the way for a counter-revolution.

Three parties with such conflicting aims made a sufficiently unhappy family, but they are far from representing all the cross-currents that distracted the legislators. There were minor divisions which frequently baffled all calculations regarding the fate of a measure. There were little cliques attached to this or that prominent personage, either from personal interest or from clan or family feeling, who were ready to vote as he might bid them. And the main parties were not always of one mind regarding the measures before the House. We find even the Ministers of State not infrequently in collision, and doing their best to checkmate each other, and it is curious to read in their reports to the authorities in London their mutual recriminations with the object of shifting the blame from their own shoulders. Nor did the Presbyterians always look in one way; for, as we have seen, one section of them put the Church before the State, and the other the State before the Church. As for the Jacobite party, it was Lockhart's bitter complaint that its divisions rendered it impotent, and that it could put no trust in the steadiness and consistency of its leaders.

The history of a Parliament thus composed could hardly fail to be a history of perpetual bickerings, of abortive bills, of compromises on the part of the government, of stolen victories, of discreditable party tactics. And such a history in great measure it is, yet through all the dust of controversy we see the great issues that were at stake and the conflict of opinions gradually focussing in the one supreme event. The Parliament that now met was to sit during three sessions, divisible into two periods by the main concerns that occupied it. In the first two years the central debate between the Ministry and the Opposition turned on the Act of Security which, passed by the House in its first session, received the royal sanction at the close of the second. By this measure Scotland threw down the gauntlet to England, and England's response was so effective that it changed the relations between the two kingdoms. As the result of England's action, the Scottish Estates were driven to accept the less of two evils—the overture of union in preference to the ruin of national trade. During its last session, therefore, the absorbing business of the Scottish Parliament was the effectuating of the Treaty of Union in its successive stages. In what remains of the present lecture, I shall deal with the first of the two periods— that, namely, in which the Act of Security was the main issue, and in dealing with it I shall refer to other matters only so far as they illustrate the history of that act.

II

We have first to note that the Ministry chosen in connexion with the new Parliament was differently composed from its predecessor. As was to be expected from the political sympathies of Nottingham and Godolphin, whose hands were now strengthened by the Tory majority in the House of Commons, the change consisted in the removal of certain of the more ardent Whigs, whose places were given to men whom it was thought desirable to conciliate. That zealous Presbyterian, the Earl of Marchmont, was deprived of the Chancellorship, which was assigned to Seafield as likely to prove a safer President of a turbulent assembly. The Secretaryship, which Seafield had held in the previous year, was given to the Earl of Cromartie, who in communications to Godolphin had assured him that the only means of salvation for Scotland was an unmixed Tory Ministry.[1] Queensberry was continued in the office of Royal Commissioner as likely to be most acceptable to all parties, and it was Seafield's charge to keep watch over him. But the most notable new member of the Ministry was one who throughout the whole reign was an object of suspicion to the English statesmen interested in Scottish affairs. This was the Marquis of Atholl, who, though he had taken a firm stand for the Revolution and had held office under William, was regarded by the Jacobites as secretly a friend of the exiled family. It was against Queensberry's will that he was given office—that of Lord Privy Seal, but Seafield had recommended him and for excellent reasons. Atholl, it is to be noted, was one of the great magnates of the Highlands, and might prove the most useful of friends or the most dangerous of enemies. But what specially influenced Seafield in recommending him for office was the fact that his authority would go far to win Jacobite support for the measures of the government. Atholl was a hot-headed

---

[1] Sir George Mackenzie, Viscount Tarbet, was made Secretary on Nov. 21, 1702, and Earl of Cromartie on Jan. 1, 1703. His communications to Godolphin on the state of parties are in the Brit. Mus. Add. MSS. 29587.

Highlander, and his speeches in the House, we are told, were often choked with passion, but Queensberry, whom he detested, had the means of holding him in check. He had petitioned the queen for a dukedom, and he had been given to hope that he would receive the honour, though not till the close of the session, and from his own letters to Godolphin we can see how Queensberry played with him.[1] We have now before us the four men—Queensberry, Seafield, Hamilton, and the Marquis of Atholl (soon to be Duke of Atholl)[2] —who from the beginning to the end of the reign were to be most influential in directing the course of events. There were others who at particular moments played conspicuous parts, but during the reign as a whole these four claim the first place. Of the four it was the Chancellor Seafield who was the central figure throughout the session. It was known that he was deepest in the counsels of Nottingham and Godolphin, and that it was by his advice that the new Scottish Ministry had been formed. His great stroke, on which he plumed himself, had been the securing of Atholl, by whose influence he hoped to win the Jacobite support for the government interest. After Seafield, Atholl came next in importance, as on his action votes frequently depended. On the whole

---

[1] Seafield writes as follows to Godolphin regarding his dealings with Atholl: ʻI do believe that if it had not been that I have pleased him [Atholl] and taken measures with him and the Cavalier party, they had been prevailed on to join with the opposers, and so there had been no possibility of carrying her Majesty's affairs.'— Add. MSS. Brit. Mus. 28055, f. 48.

[2] Atholl's patent for the Dukedom had passed the seals, but Queensberry did not put it in his hands till the following October, after the close of the session.—Add. MSS. Brit. Mus. 28055, f. 64.

he fulfilled Seafield's expectation, though he often
took a way of his own and even incurred the displeasure of the queen by his differences with his
colleagues. The Duke of Hamilton, though he made
himself prominent in altercation and debate, had not
the large following he had led in the preceding Parliament—the Country Party strictly so called being now
reduced to the number of fifteen. 'Seafield', Harley
wrote to Godolphin, 'seems in his distribution of
parties to leave none to Duke Hamilton.'[1] Queensberry, though he represented the sovereign, held only
a second place to Seafield, who was known to be
in closer touch with the Court, and, moreover, he was
comparatively impotent in a Ministry in which Atholl
and others of his party were in constant collusion
with Seafield.

There was no such sensational event in the session as
the withdrawal of Hamilton and his party, but passions
rose even higher, and there were scenes when the
House became a mere shouting mob; 'we were
often', records one of its members, 'we were often
in the form of a Polish diet with our swords in our
hands, or at least our hands at our swords'. 'In all
this struggle', he adds, and the comment might be
applied to other representative assemblies, 'in all this
struggle there was no great good done, so that I am
persuaded we had spent our time at home more to
the benefit of the nation.'[2] So he wrote as a supporter of the Court Party, and the English managers
in London cordially shared his opinion. And, in point

---

[1] Add. MSS. Brit. Mus. 28055, f. 5.
[2] Hume of Crossrig, *Diary*, p. 49.

of fact, the animating spirit of the Estates as a body, from the beginning to the close of the session, was hostility to England and antipathy to any form of union.

So far as the Court was concerned, there were two main objects for which the Estates had been summoned. The one was to have the late Parliament legalized; the other, to obtain supply. The legalizing of the late Parliament was of prime necessity for Anne, since it was by the sanction of that assembly that she was sovereign of Scotland. This measure Queensberry had no difficulty in carrying, as no party except the extreme Jacobites had any interest in opposing it. It was very different in the case of supply, the power to grant or refuse which afforded the only means at the command of the Estates for making terms with the government. All the members who desired the maintenance of the Revolution Settlement, and they were the majority, were aware that in the interests of that settlement supply was urgently necessary. In the previous year England had declared war with France, and it was among the probable chances of that war that France would strike at England through Scotland—England's 'back-door', as it was significantly described. As at a later period both nations were made to learn, a French invasion of Scotland in concert with the Jacobites at home might seriously imperil the existing *régime*. Nevertheless, so embittered was the general feeling of the House at the managers in England, that, as we shall see, Queensberry, with all his arts, did not succeed in extracting a penny for the maintenance of the troops necessary for the country's defence.

The measures actually passed by the House showed the same hostile attitude to the government. In an act for the 'securing of the true Protestant religion and Presbyterian government' was implied a distinct monition to the queen herself, whose Episcopalian sympathies had betrayed her into an indiscreet action. She had addressed a letter to the Privy Council expressly urging toleration to Episcopalians, and the purport of her letter had become publicly known. The result was a riot in Edinburgh on such a scale that the magistrates were unable to suppress it, and the example of Edinburgh was followed by the mob of Glasgow. In the House itself it was clamoured that the objectionable letter should be read, and, though the Ministers urged that this would be an insult to the queen, they found themselves forced to yield the point. Expressly against the wish of the queen, also, there was passed another act which boded ill for the future relations of the two kingdoms. Since the Union of the Crowns the successive sovereigns had never consulted the Scottish Estates in their declarations of war, yet they had exacted from Scotland her proportional quota of men and money. In view of the great war in which England was now engaged, this was assuredly a grievance which the least sensitive of patriots might resent. It was with justifiable patriotism, therefore, that an act was carried ordaining that no successor of the reigning sovereign should declare a war involving Scotland without consulting her representatives.[1] In the same spirit of defiance was passed another act which, be it noted,

---

[1] *Acts of Parl. of Scot.*, xi, p. 107.

had the support of both Jacobites and Whigs. By England's war with France her trade with that country had been interrupted, but this was no reason, it was urged, that Scotland should be a sufferer for her sake. By a measure, known as the Wine Act, therefore, it was made legal to import all foreign wines and liquors from all countries—France included.[1]

The conflicting interests of the two kingdoms were signally illustrated in the case of a question that vitally concerned the future of both. By the Act of Settlement of 1701 the English Parliament had devolved the Crown on the Electress Sophia and her descendants, but to this arrangement the Scottish Estates had never given their sanction. It was of the first importance, therefore, that this sanction should be obtained : 'anybody may judge', Godolphin wrote to Atholl, 'that neither that nor this Kingdom can be very secure when they are not under the same succession, and in this both reason and experience seem to agree.'[2] What is remarkable is that, with the exception of such members of the House as were tied to the Court, all parties were equally resolute against following the example of England : 'in anything against the English succession', Seafield told Godolphin, 'our opposit pairtie are strongest.'[3] We can understand how the Jacobites should oppose as a death-stroke to their hopes an arrangement that would definitely debar the

---

[1] *Acts of Parl. of Scot.*, xi, p. 112. It was against Anne's will that these two acts were sanctioned, but Queensberry had represented to her that, if her sanction were refused, there would be no hope of supply.

[2] *Athole Papers*, Hist. MSS. Com., Report XII, App. III, p. 61.

[3] *Seafield Letters*, Add. MSS. Brit. Mus. 28055, f. 52.

succession of the Pretender, but what is singular is that, with the exception of a few ultra-Presbyterians, it was equally abhorrent to the Whigs.   One of the most violent scenes in a tumultuous session occurred when the Earl of Marchmont proposed a measure in favour of the Hanoverian succession.   That the Whigs took this line seems explicable only by the fact that antagonism to England at all points seemed to them for the moment the true national policy.

We come to the portentous birth of the session—the Act of Security which, meant as a defiance to England, was by the irony of circumstance to be the immediate occasion of the Treaty of Union.   It was brought forth amid throes which might be truly described as revolutionary.   As it finally emerged, it was the outcome of a conflict of opinion which raged throughout the greater part of the session, and it is to be regarded as the deliberate expression of the attitude towards England of the great majority of the House.   There was a numerous section in the House, indeed, to whom it seemed a weak and ineffective measure which afforded no guarantee that Scotland would be any better off in her relations to her tyrannical ally.   The leader of this minority was one of the notable figures of the period, and of all his contemporaries he is the best known to his countrymen of to-day.   This was Andrew Fletcher of Saltoun, whose chequered career sufficiently avouches his energetic character.   He had begun his public life by a bold arraignment of the policy of Lauderdale, was accessory to the Rye-house Plot, joined Monmouth's expedition, during which he pistolled a bully who insulted him, fought against the Turks, and eventually returned to his native country as a supporter of William. But William's rule in Scotland by no means satisfied him, and he became one of the most prominent members of the Country Party in its opposition to the Court. A persistent speaker in the House, the burden of his oratory was that, since the union of the Crowns, Scotland had been a mere satrapy of England and that all the miseries from which she was suffering were due to that fact. He had none of the qualities of a political leader, and did not aspire to be one, but his sincerity and disinterestedness were recognized by all parties, and he seldom spoke without setting the House aflame. By more moderate men he was regarded as a visionary, an Ishmael, who was out of his place and time. His head was so teeming with schemes of government, so it was said of him, that he would have been the first man to be hanged if they had been realized, as he would have been the first to suggest their alteration. And his outer was in accord with his inner man; as he is described by a contemporary, he was 'a low thin man, brown complexion, full of fire, with a stern, sour look'.

The contention of Fletcher and those who supported him was that only by limiting the prerogative of the sovereign was there any hope that the country would be preserved from the malign influence of England. To accomplish this object, therefore, he brought forward a list of no fewer than twelve 'limitations' or restrictions on the royal authority which should be embodied in the Act of Security, and which should take effect on the accession of a new sovereign.[1] The

---

[1] The most important of the 'limitations' proposed by Fletcher were as follow: that there shall be annual elections; that the king

outcome of these limitations would have been that the monarchy must have been transformed into a republic, and for once all the Ministers were of one mind in their opposition to Fletcher's proposals. It was the crucial issue of the session, and the Court followed the protracted contest with undisguised anxiety. It was now that Godolphin wrote the words to which reference has already been made. ' But we are now in so criticall a conjuncture with respect to other nations, that all Europe must in some measure bee affected by the good or ill ending of the Parliament of Scotland.' [1] It was in connexion with Fletcher's proposal to embody his limitations in the Act of Security that Atholl did a notable service to the government : it was only by the aid of the Jacobites who followed his lead that the limitations were eventually excluded. [2] And the fact that they were excluded is a determining circumstance in the relations of the two kingdoms. It was only out of dire necessity that in the end the royal sanction was given to the act, but if the limitations, which would virtually have made Scotland an independent republic, had formed part of it, Anne and her advisers could in no circumstances have yielded their consent to its becoming law. What, in that event, would have been the result on the relations of the two kingdoms it is impossible to say, but in any case the history of the

shall sanction all laws passed by the Estates ; that without the consent of Parliament the king shall not have the power of making peace and war ; and that, if any king shall infringe these conditions, he shall be declared by the Estates to have forfeited the Crown.

[1] *Seafield Papers*, Hist. MSS. Com., Report XIV, App. Part III, p. 199.

[2] Add. MSS. Brit. Mus. 28055, f. 44.

Union, if union would actually have taken place, would have been different from what it was.

Even in its final form the act was sufficiently unpalatable to Anne and her Ministers. By its terms the Estates, twenty days after the death of the reigning sovereign without issue, were to name a successor who should be at once a Protestant and a descendant of the house of Stewart. Whoever this successor might be, he or she must not be the person designated by the Parliament of England except under conditions that secured to Scotland complete freedom of government, of religion, and of trade. And another clause in the act showed that it was meant as no idle threat: landholders and burghs were required to provide all able-bodied men with arms and to hold a monthly levy for exercise and discipline.[1] Neither Anne nor her Ministers were prepared to sanction a measure, the effect of which must be the eventual severance of the crowns, but they were placed in an embarrassing dilemma. They were given to understand by all the queen's servants in Scotland that they must choose between two evils: they must either sanction the objectionable bill, or forfeit the supplies necessary to maintain a military force adequate to defend Scotland from internal revolt and foreign invasion. Despite the advice of the Scottish Ministers, they chose to dispense with supply. So ended the first session of the new Parliament, and in the opinion of all observers its proceedings in its future meetings were as little likely to make for peace and amity between the two nations.[2]

[1] *Acts of Parl. of Scot.*, xi, pp. 69, 74.

[2] An interesting account of the proceedings of this session is given in the letters of the Duke of Atholl. See App. I.

III

What, with this prospect before them, would be the policy of Anne's English advisers ? In another session of the same Parliament supply would in all probability be refused if the Act of Security did not receive the royal sanction. But it was no longer possible, as it had been in the reign of Charles II, to let years elapse between the meetings of the Estates. Had this policy been tried, all parties would have combined and protested, sword in hand, that Scotland must go her own way. Moreover, supply was indispensable if Anne were to retain Scotland as part of her dominion, since the country would never consent to its defensive forces being maintained by English money. Anne and her Ministers, therefore, realized that before a year elapsed they must face another session of the intractable assembly.

In the interval there happened one of those sensational incidents which so abundantly diversify the course of Scottish history. It is the incident which was known in England as the Scots Plot, but in Scotland as the Queensberry Plot, from the chief person associated with it. We are now concerned with the Plot only so far as it affected the relations of the two kingdoms. The prime mover in the business was one who bears an evil name in the national annals. He was Simon Lovat, afterwards the Lord Fraser of Lovat, who was executed for his share in the Rising of 1745. He had been attainted and exiled for a scandalous deed, and had gone to France, where he wormed himself into the

councils of the exiled House. Returning to Scotland
as their accredited agent, so he alleged, he communi-
cated to Queensberry the secrets of the mission with
which he had been charged. There was a plot, he told,
in which the Duke of Atholl was the principal agent,
and the object of it was to effect a rising in the Highlands in favour of the Pretender. And not only Atholl
was implicated, but many of the Scottish nobility, and
among them Hamilton, Seafield, and the Secretary of
State, the Earl of Cromartie. Queensberry knew the
character of Lovat, and suspected his tale from the
first. Nevertheless, it placed him in an awkward
dilemma. Everybody knew that there were traffickings
between the Court at St. Germains and many of the
most prominent men in Scotland, and there was probably some foundation for Lovat's story. But without
better evidence than Lovat's it was a risky proceeding
to incriminate statesmen who were known to be his
personal enemies. On the other hand, the existing
defences of the country were so inadequate that a
foreign invasion in concert with an internal revolt
would be a serious peril. As the result of an Act of
Indemnity, passed in the spring of 1703, many Jacobites had returned from exile, and some of them were
known to be emissaries of the Pretender. For the
protection of the whole of the sea-coast there were
only three frigates, insufficiently manned and equipped.
As for the army, we have a description of it from the
hand of Lieutenant-General George Ramsay, Commander of the forces in Scotland. It consisted nominally of 3,000 men, of whom 120 formed the garrison
of the Castle of Edinburgh, 400 that of Stirling, and
40 that of Dumbarton. Besides these garrisons, there

were three[1] companies for the defence of the Highlands, but on them, in Ramsay's opinion, no dependence could be placed in the event of a rising. Moreover, certain of the officers of highest rank in the army had by their votes in Parliament shown that they were no friends of the existing government.[2]

In these circumstances it was a public duty that Queensberry, as the royal representative in Scotland, should communicate what he had heard to the sovereign. Whatever may have been his motive, he took this step, and he received a reply from the English Secretary of State, the Earl of Nottingham, to the effect that the queen was pleased with his action and instructing him to make further use of Lovat for the discovery of what truth might be in his allegations. It is at this point that the affair became a matter of importance in the relations of the two countries. At the instance of the English Ministers the question of the Plot was laid before the Parliament, and the House of Lords, mainly consisting of Whigs, appointed a special committee to examine the correspondence produced by Fraser. After an inquiry lasting several months the committee gave in its report, which was adopted by the House. According to that report there had been a dangerous conspiracy with the object of bringing in the pretended Prince of Wales, and nothing had given more encouragement to the conspiracy than the fact that the crown of Scotland had not, like that of England, been settled in favour of the Princess

---

[1] A third company had been added since the beginning of Anne's reign.

[2] *Letters of Lieutenant-General Ramsay*, Add. MSS. Brit. Mus. 28055, f. 98.

Sophia and her heirs. The queen, therefore, the report urged, should be advised to adopt such methods as seemed most effective to settle the Scottish succession at the earliest date. This report, sanctioned by the Lords, was to be a dominating fact in influencing the proceedings of the Scottish Estates in their approaching session. It was resented by all the members except those who, either from principle or personal interest, took their orders from the Court. That the Lords should have meddled with an affair in which Scotland was mainly concerned, was regarded as a national insult, aggravated by the fact that the English Ministers persistently refused to send down the incriminating documents for examination by the Scottish Parliament. But the head and front of the Lords' offence was that they presumed to dictate to Scotland the policy she must follow. It will be seen, therefore, that the Plot was an untoward incident which might well have had even more serious consequences than it actually involved.

The immediate and inevitable result of the Plot was a confusion of parties in which former divisions were for the time forgotten. Lovat's communications had incriminated members both of the Jacobite and Country parties, who were thus bound by a common interest to self-defence against Queensberry and his following. With this object, therefore, their leaders held common councils, the results of which were to appear in the approaching session of the Estates. It is Lockhart who gives the fullest account of them, and his narrative is on the whole corroborated by such contemporary documents as we possess. The first proceeding was an arrangement made by the

Jacobites with Atholl, Seafield, and Cromartie, all of whom still held office, but who had also been pointed at as accessory to the Plot.   In the interests of the Jacobites they were to proceed to London and there do their utmost to checkmate Queensberry.   It was Marlborough and Godolphin who now took the chief interest in Scottish affairs, and Lockhart bitingly comments on the servility of the opposing Scottish parties to these two Ministers, who treated them, he says, 'with no more civility than one gentleman pays another's valet-de-chambre'.

While the three representatives of the Jacobites were thus dancing attendance on the Court, Hamilton, who was also charged with being in the Plot, took further measures to baffle his enemy, Queensberry. He convened a meeting of the Jacobites and the Country Party in Edinburgh, which agreed to send up three other representatives to London to further their interests.   The three who were chosen were all members of the Country Party, as known Jacobites were not likely to be acceptable at Court.   They were the Earls of Roxburgh and Rothes and George Baillie of Jerviswoode, all of whom were to play notable parts in the future.   Their instructions were to represent to her majesty that the Plot had been vamped up with the sole object of ruining certain of her good subjects in Scotland, and that it was necessary that the Estates should meet at the earliest date to right the wrong and to pass measures in the interest of the country.   To the indignation of the Jacobites all three were gained over by Godolphin, who had already decided on a measure which he meant to have laid before the Scottish Parliament.

As things now stood between the two countries, the measure which was in Godolphin's mind was of vital importance for both. By the Claim of Right passed by the Scottish Convention at the Revolution, the Scottish crown had been settled on the heirs of Mary and Anne, and, failing heirs to both, on the heirs of William. In this settlement there was no distinct provision for the succession of the House of Hanover, and it was Godolphin's object to procure an act from the Scottish Estates which should leave no dubiety on the point. Rothes, Roxburgh, and Baillie agreed to take office in a Ministry which should endeavour to pass such an act, but on one condition. We have seen that in the late session of the Estates, Fletcher and the Country Party had passionately urged certain restrictions on the royal prerogative which should take effect on the death of Anne. Unless the demand were at least partially met, Rothes and his friends knew that it would be impossible to carry an Act of Succession. The condition they attached to their accepting office, therefore, was the confirmation of an act which had been passed by the Covenanting Parliament of 1641 and sanctioned by Charles I. By the terms of that act, all Officers of State, Privy Councillors, and Judges were to be chosen by the king, but 'with the advice and approbation' of the Estates. On the same terms Godolphin secured the support of two other important persons to his measure—the Marquis of Tweeddale, a prominent member of the Country Party, and James Johnstone, a staunch Revolutionist, who had been Secretary of State under William, and was the special bugbear of the Jacobites. In gaining the support of Rothes and his friends, Godolphin obtained another advantage, for by their influence a section was detached from the Country Party which, under the name of the New Party, could be reckoned upon to vote for government measures. But this advantage was more than counterbalanced by another party arrangement which throws a strange light on the time. The Jacobites bargained with their enemy Queensberry that they would not raise the question of the Plot in the coming session if he and his following would join hands with them in opposing the proposed Act of Succession.

When, on July 6, 1704, the Estates again sat, Anne and her English Ministers were in the full assurance that their main object in summoning them— the passing of an act settling the crown on the Electress Sophia and her heirs—would be carried by an ample majority. Every precaution had been taken to ensure this result. The Ministry of the previous year had been radically changed. Queensberry, as objectionable to the majority of the House on account of the Plot, was deprived of the office of Royal Commissioner, which was given to the Marquis of Tweeddale, the leader of the New Party. Atholl retained the office of Lord Privy Seal, and Johnstone, who had been Godolphin's chief adviser during the preceding months, was made Lord Clerk Register. The accommodating Seafield was continued in the office of Chancellor. Titles were freely given to persons who might prove useful, and promises of good things were held out to others on condition of acceptable service.[1]

---

[1] *Instructions to Seafield*, Hist. MSS. Com., Fourteenth Report, App. Part III, pp. 194-5.

The session had not well begun before the Ministers discovered that they had gravely miscalculated their chances. They found themselves face to face with an assemblage whose hostility to the proposed Act of Succession displayed itself with increasing intensity as the session proceeded. Arrayed against them were all the three dukes—Queensberry, Atholl, Hamilton, —and the ardent Fletcher. Queensberry did not appear in the House, but through his intermediaries he influenced the Revolution Whigs against a measure which on their own principles they should have welcomed. Atholl, though he held office, proved a thorn in the side of his colleagues. He knew when he took office that the passing of the Act of Succession was the chief business with which the Ministry was entrusted, yet he did his best to thwart them at every turn. In the case of Hamilton there were personal reasons why he should dislike the measure.[1] As has already been said, his ancestors in every successive reign since that of Mary had been suspected of aiming at the crown. But to none of them had the chances of realizing their ambition been more favourable than they were to their living representative. In the event of Scotland breaking away from England, which the relations of the two countries seemed to make every day more probable, she would almost be shut up to the choice of him as her king.

[1] Hamilton's ambiguous action is perhaps best explained on the supposition that he was aiming at the Crown. In this view, also, his associations with the Jacobites would be explained, as he would naturally desire to attach them to his interest. He was constantly in straits for money, and his action was further checked by his fear of losing his estates in England.

He was of royal blood, a Protestant, and, as the leader
of the Country Party, which represented the national
aspirations, the most generally popular of all the
political leaders of the day. Perfectly disinterested,
on the other hand, was the opposition of Fletcher. His
one panacea for all the ills from which his country was
suffering was a government which should give effect
to the nation's will—whether monarchy or republic was
indifferent to him. Against an opposition concentrated in these four men, the Ministry found itself help-
less, and in their reports to the managers in London
they made frank confession of their impotence.

In a series of unprinted letters to Godolphin, Johnstone, the Clerk Register, to whom, as we have seen,
the charge of the queen's measure had been entrusted,
vividly describes the painful experiences of himself and
his colleagues. Two days after the session had begun,
he writes that matters were in a very bad way and
that there was a general and growing aversion to
the queen's measure. Later, he wrote that he had
nothing but government defeats to report, and that
it was a prevalent conviction that at heart the queen
herself did not wish the measure to pass.[1] And not
only in the House, but in the world outside of it,
general sympathy was with the Opposition. Hamilton
was attended by cheering crowds on his way from the
Parliament House to Holyrood, while it was at the risk
of his life that Johnstone walked the streets, and stones
were thrown through his wife's window.[2]

---

[1] By other authorities of the time the queen's dislike to settling
the succession is frequently mentioned.

[2] *Letters of J. Johnstone, Lord Clerk Register of Scotland*, Add.
MSS. Brit. Mus. 28055, ff. 90, 103, 107, 114, 118, 126, 128.

As the result of the session, the government found itself thwarted at all points. Its great measure—the settling of the crown in favour of Hanover—which it had confidently hoped to pass, never had a chance of passing. The main reason urged against it was that, though it might be in the interests of England, it would do no good to Scotland. It gave, for example, no guarantee that in the matter of trade Scotland would be better treated by England. Therefore Hamilton contended that a treaty which would give equality of commercial privileges to both countries should precede an act for settling the succession. Hamilton's motion for such a treaty killed the government measure, but it did not pass into a formal act. There was a proposal, indeed, to appoint commissioners to negotiate a treaty, but the proposal did not take definite shape— to the regret of Lockhart, as at that moment the Jacobites might have secured a larger representation on the commission than they eventually did at a later period.

The defeat of the one measure which the Ministry had been specially chosen to carry was a rude blow for Godolphin, but a more staggering one followed. Supply was an imperative necessity if the government of the country was to be carried on. But when supply was asked, the Ministers were told that they would have it only on one condition—the queen must give the sanction she had refused in the previous year to the Act of Security. Strangely enough, the Commissioner had received no instructions as to how he should act in the event of this alternative arising. Before he could give his reply, therefore, he had to communicate with London, and with one voice he and his colleagues urged Godolphin to give way. By advising the queen to refuse her sanction Godolphin ran the risk of raising a rebellion in Scotland; by advising her to grant it, he was hazarding his position as an English Minister. He chose the latter alternative; the Commissioner was empowered to touch the momentous act with the sceptre (the symbol of the royal sanction)[1]; and supply was granted for six months. Not content with the expression of the national will implied in the Act of Security, on the last day of the session the Estates took another emphatic step. They voted an address to the queen in which she was plainly told that the intermeddling of the House of Lords in the affairs of Scotland was an insult to the nation.[2]

With the passing of the Act of Security, the first stage in the history of the Union Parliament ends. By that act, as was fully understood, the two nations were 'divided by law', and, as a clause in the same act bore that Scotland was prepared to support her protest by arms, he would have been a sanguine observer who would have predicted that in the course of little more than two years the unequally-yoked kingdoms would find a basis for a union in which their reciprocal interests would form the permanent bond. How this union came to be effected by the assembly which apparently had done its utmost to prevent it, will be the subject of the two following lectures.

[1] In the act, as it was sanctioned, the clause relating to a commercial treaty with England was omitted.

[2] *Acts of Parl. of Scot.*, xi, p. 204. See App. II for an account of the proceedings of the session by Johnstone in his letters to Godolphin.

LECTURE IV

SUCCESSION OR UNION?

I

It was pointed out in the last lecture how the Act of Security, now that it had received the sanction of the crown, fundamentally changed the relations of the two kingdoms. In his *History of the Union* De Foe clearly defined the new situation. The act, he says, had made two things plain: (1) that Scotland was resolved to have the bestowal of her crown in her own hands, and (2) that only on certain conditions would she give it to the successor of Anne chosen by England. This ultimatum, De Foe adds, 'effectually settled and declared the independency of Scotland, and put her into a posture fit to be treated with, either by England or by any other nation'.[1] It was, in truth, the menace of the second alternative—the possibility of Scotland one day becoming an independent and hostile kingdom—which convinced English statesmen that Scotland could no longer be treated as a mere dependency. For the first time since the Union of the Crowns, that is, for a full century, the English Parliament seriously addressed itself to find a settlement which would unite the two nations by a bond of common interests and common aims.

In England the time was not opportune for the calm discussion of healing measures. The House of Commons was still that Tory assembly which had been

[1] *History of the Union* (1709), Part I, pp. 52-3.

returned in the first year of the reign, but it was now about to meet in its last session, and, in view of an approaching general election, party passions were at their height. In the conflict of faction the affairs of Scotland were to play an important part. It was Godolphin who was responsible for the pass to which things had come in that country, and at this moment he was the object of a concentrated attack by the Tories for his dallying with the Whigs. And in their attack on Godolphin for his Scottish policy the Tory leaders had the support of English public opinion behind them. The wildest rumours regarding the intentions of the Scots came to be current in the country. They had bought 30,000 stand of arms in Holland; they had laid in a store of 10,000 barrels of powder; they were arming 60,000 men, and France would, of course, be at their back.[1] An untoward coincidence increased the difficulties of Godolphin's position. A few days after the royal sanction had been given to the Act of Security, came the news of Marlborough's victory at Blenheim, and, in view of this national triumph, Godolphin's yielding to the clamour of a turbulent people appeared to be a weak and contemptible surrender.

It was in this state of English public opinion with regard to Scottish affairs that Parliament met on November 29, 1704. It was the House of Lords that first took up the business of Scotland. The Tory leaders who conducted the attack on Godolphin's Scottish policy were Lord Haversham and the Earls of Nottingham and Rochester; the leaders on the other side were Lords Somers, Halifax, and Wharton. The queen herself,

[1] De Foe, *History of the Union*, p. 54.

doubtless to give her countenance to Godolphin, was present during this and other debates, sitting on a bench near the fire on account of the cold. Haversham opened the debate in a speech, the heads of which have been preserved. The state of affairs in Scotland, he said, was such as to demand the serious consideration of the House, and that state of affairs was the result of an ill-judged policy. A 'motley Ministry' had been set up in that country, which had completely failed to carry an act settling the succession—the passing of which was the special object for which it had been chosen. Moreover, it had failed to prevent the passing of the Act of Security, which was virtually an Act of Exclusion, and which ordained the Scottish nation to put itself under arms. 'There are two matters of all troubles', he continued, 'much discontent, and great poverty; and whoever will now look into Scotland will find them both in that kingdom. It is certain the nobility and gentry of Scotland are as learned and as brave as any nation in Europe can boast of; and these are generally discontented. And as to the common people, they are very numerous and very stout, but very poor. And who is the man that can answer what such a multitude so armed, so disciplined, with such leaders, may do, especially since opportunities do so much alter men from themselves? And there will never be wanting all the promises and all the assistance that France can give '.[1]

The object of the Tory leaders was to have the Act of Security condemned by the House, and with this object they moved that the act should be read.

[1] Rapin, *History of England*, continued by Tindal, vol. xxi, pp. 109-11.

On the ground of inexpediency the motion was opposed
by Somers, Wharton, and Godolphin.   Godolphin ad-
mitted that the state of things in Scotland was not
what he would have wished, and that the Act of
Security had 'an untowardly aspect'.   In the circumstances however, he said, there would have been more
immediate danger in refusing than in granting the
royal sanction to the act, and, moreover, he significantly added, he thought there was a remedy.   What
that remedy was to be was indicated in a motion by
Somers which doubtless had been concerted in conjunction with Godolphin.   Somers's motion was that
the House should proceed by way of a bill, the terms
of which would convince the Scots that, if they chose
to set up an independent kingdom, they would themselves be the greatest sufferers ; and with the object
of preparing such a bill he proposed that the House
should go into a grand committee.[1]

Somers's motion was made on December 6, and on
the 11th the Earl of Sunderland submitted the heads
of a bill approved by the grand committee, which
eventually took shape as an act and received the
sanction of the House.   But besides passing this act,
the Lords took another step which showed their
serious disquiet at the attitude of Scotland.   In a body
they presented an address to the queen in which they
earnestly urged her to make provision for the safety
of the kingdom pending the operation of the act they
were engaged in preparing.   Newcastle should be put
in a condition of defence ; the port of Tynemouth

---

[1] *Letters of Mr. Vernon to the Duke of Shrewsbury*, 1st and 8th
Dec., 1704, printed in App. to Somerville's *Hist. of Great Britain
during the reign of Queen Anne* (1798), pp. 616–19.

should be secured; the fortifications of Berwick, Carlisle, and Hull strengthened; regular troops should be posted in the North of England and Ireland, and the militia of the northern counties should be made ready for service.[1]

Meantime the House of Commons had also been busy with the affairs of Scotland, though it addressed itself to them in a cooler temper than the Lords. While the House of Lords was mainly Whig, the Commons were mainly Tory, and they were not specially zealous for a Scottish Act of Succession which would settle the crown on the House of Hanover. Public opinion, however, demanded that something should be done to show the Scots that they would have most to lose in the event of their breaking away from England. A bill similar in effect to that of the Lords was therefore introduced, but while it was still under discussion the bill of the Lords was sent down to the Commons. To the Lords' bill a novel objection was taken; among its clauses was one which threatened money-penalties, and which the Commons, therefore, regarded as an infringement of their privilege as guardians of the national purse. Rejecting the Lords' bill on this ground, they sent their own to the Upper House, where, on February 14, 1705, it was passed without a single amendment.

The act was a rousing reminder to the Scots that two could play at the game in which they were engaged. The title of the act is itself a significant commentary on the situation that had arisen between the two kingdoms. It was entitled, 'An Act for the effectual securing the Kingdom of England from the

[1] *Journals of the House of Lords*, xvii. 596, 607.

apparent dangers that may arise from several acts lately passed in the Parliament of Scotland.' Yet the first and principal clause of the act was conceived in no hostile spirit. It enacted that the queen should nominate commissioners for England with powers to treat with commissioners authorized by the Parliament of Scotland regarding such a union of the two kingdoms as would tend to the 'common good' of both. It was an addendum to the third clause that brought the Scots face to face with the situation which had been created by their Act of Security. Should no treaty be effected by December 25, 1705, the addendum declared that after that date these consequences should follow : all Scotsmen, except such as were settled in England, would be treated as aliens ; no horses, arms, or ammunition would be supplied to Scotland from England; and Scottish cattle, linen, and coals would be excluded both from England and Ireland.[1]

The threat of an alternative between union and loss of trade was a sobering reality for every Scotsman who had his country's well-being at heart. Coals, linen, and cattle were her chief exports, and three-fourths of the trade in these commodities was done with England. Scottish statesmen of all parties fully realized the gravity of the situation. It was with anxious vigilance that those of them who were in London followed the proceedings of the Parliament in connexion with the Alien Act, as it came to be called. 'Some talk here of discharging our cattle being brought in ; if that's done, we are ruined.' So wrote the Earl of Roxburgh on the first rumour of the Parliament's intentions. A week later he writes :

---

[1] *Statutes at Large*, iv. 78–9.

' Pray let me have certain information whether we can export our cattle and linen elsewhere or not to our advantage; for we cannot subsist without exporting our product. . . .' At a further stage of the Parliament's action he writes in a mood still more grave. ' What will become of our affairs between the House of Lords and the House of Commons is very uncertain, but I am throughly convinc'd that, if we do not go into the Succession or an Union very soon, conquest will certainly be upon the first peace.'[1]

II

In the letter of Roxburgh last quoted there is a passage which ominously marks another occasion of misunderstanding between the two nations, already, as it might seem, on the point of drawing the sword. ' The East India ship', he wrote, ' makes a great noise here. . . . It is a great misfortune, and, indeed, our misfortunes are many.' Roxburgh might have used a stronger expression, for the affair of the East India ship threatened more than mere misfortune : it threatened an international calamity. Under less mutual provocation nations have many times gone to war, and that war was not the issue of the exasperation of the two peoples is signal proof of the constraining forces that made for their union. With the minuter details of the affair we are not now concerned, as it is only in its larger import that we are interested. Its immediate results were the same as in the case of the Queensberry Plot : it was a main cause of a change

[1] *Correspondence of George Baillie*, Ban. Club, 1842, pp. 13, 19, 28.

in the Scottish Ministry, and it raised to frenzy the jealous antagonism of Englishman and Scot. And it emphasizes another fact which had an important bearing on the prospects of a Treaty of Union. What the story of the whole affair appeared to indicate was that, if a violent crisis arose, a Scottish Ministry could not resist public opinion. Such a crisis came at a later day, when a Treaty of Union was actually under consideration; and it was the hope and the endeavour of the statesmen who opposed it to defeat it by appeal to the populace. In connexion with the India ship we shall see that the commands of the queen were disregarded by the Privy Council of Scotland out of sheer terror of the mob.

The story of the ship is briefly as follows. A Scottish vessel, named the *Annandale,* was seized in the Thames by the English East India Company on the ground of some breach of its privileges. The *Annandale* belonged to the Scottish African Company whose Darien enterprise English merchants had done much to ruin, and this repeated proof of their jealousy of Scottish trading interests was keenly resented by the nation at large. By what was regarded as a special intervention of Providence, in August, 1704, an English ship, the *Worcester*, mistakenly supposed to belong to the offending East India Company, put into the roads of Leith, in the Firth of Forth. Without legal authority, the Secretary of the African Company, at the head of an armed party, boarded the vessel and made prisoners of the crew. Providence further intervened, for in their cups certain of the crew spoke mysteriously of deeds of piracy they had done on the high seas. As it chanced, there was a Scottish craft, the *Speedy Return*, regarding the fate of which there had been long uncertainty, and suspicion arose that it had been one of the victims of the *Worcester*. 'There are sometimes,' is De Foe's reflection on the proceedings that followed, 'there are sometimes such crises, such junctures in matters, when all things shall concur to possess, not a man, but even a nation with a belief of what at another time they would not believe even upon the same evidence.'[1] As a concession to popular clamour, the Privy Council ordered that the Captain (whose name was Green) and all his crew should be put on their trial, though the Lord Chancellor Seafield was of opinion that the trial was illegal, as no ship was specified as the victim of the accused. It is to be noted (and the point is important in view of future developments) that it was mainly the members of the New Party in the Council who insisted on the trial. On the 14th of March, 1705, seven months after the seizure of the vessel, the Court of Admiralty sat in judgement on the accused, and after a week's examination found them all guilty except one. Be it said that it was not only the mob who were convinced of the guilt of Green and his crew; responsible statesmen were of opinion that the evidence against them was conclusive. Baillie of Jerviswoode, the most influential leader of the New Party, wrote to the Secretary of State Johnstone, that 'the murder, as well as piracy, is made clear to conviction, and that it was our ship and men that were so treated'[2]; and the Earls of Leven and Annandale expressed the same opinion to Seafield.

It was on the condemnation of Green and his men

---

[1] De Foe, *op. cit.*, p. 47.   [2] Baillie, *op. cit.*, p. 65.

that the tension between the two nations reached its height. Feeling in England ran as high as in Scotland. No Scotsman dared show his face in the streets of London; as things were going, Johnstone wrote to Seafield, it was enough to 'make an unborn child cry'.[1] The universal opinion in England was that the condemned men were innocent, and, though in the state of public opinion in Scotland the consequences might be serious, the queen was advised to intervene. By the sentence of the Admiralty, the condemned men were to be executed in batches at intervals of a week. April 4 was the day fixed for the execution of Green and four of his crew. Before the day came, there arrived a letter from the Duke of Argyle, now Royal Commissioner, expressing the queen's pleasure that the men should be reprieved. Unfortunately, in connexion with this letter there was a double inadvertence. It came from the Royal Commissioner, whereas it should have come direct from the queen, and it was addressed to the Chancellor Seafield, whereas it ought to have been addressed to the Privy Council as a body. The difficulty occasioned was this. Had the letter come directly from the queen to the Council, its members would have had a pretext for granting a reprieve to the five condemned men which would exonerate them in the eyes of the public. As it was, they could put forward no such pretext, and accordingly, instead of granting a reprieve, they sent a petition to the queen, craving that a reprieve should not be granted.[2] A few days later came a direct communication from the queen ordering a reprieve, and the

---

[1] *Seafield Correspondence*, Scot. Hist. Soc., p. 401.

[2] *Seafield Letters*, Add. MSS. Brit. Mus. 28055, f. 350.

execution of the five men was postponed from the 4th to the 11th of April.

That 11th of April is one of the memorable days in the history of the Scottish capital, and its story is fully told in an unpublished letter of Seafield to Godolphin. On the morning of that day Seafield received a flying packet from Godolphin containing a letter from the queen and a bundle of documents proving the innocence of Green and his crew. In expectation of the packet, he had the night before requested all the Councillors in town, ten or eleven in all, to meet at his house at eight the next morning. When the Councillors appeared at the appointed hour, they reported that there were signs of an impending tumult. The streets were swarming with an excited mob, and crowds were flocking in from the surrounding country. All that could be done was to dispatch messages to the magistrates and the Commander of the Forces to warn them to be on their guard. The contents of the packet were then read, but it was resolved that no decision on them could be taken by so small a body of Councillors, who, moreover, were themselves divided in opinion. In point of fact, since the question of reprieve had arisen, not a single Minister had attended the meetings of Council—the reason being that they must either offend the queen or endanger their popularity. It was resolved, however, that to give a greater semblance of authority to their proceedings they should go in a body to the Council Chamber at Holyrood. As they made their way down the High Street and the Canongate, they were attended by excited crowds, shouting 'Justice, Justice! No Reprieve!' Arrived at the Council Chamber, after some discussion they concluded that, unless some victims were given up, it would be impossible to maintain the public peace. As supposed to be the most guilty, Captain Green and two others were selected for sacrifice that very day— the rest of the crew being reprieved till the 19th, and eventually let off, though not till the following October. On his way home in his coach, Seafield had an opportunity of realizing the state of public feeling. By the crowd in the vicinity of Holyrood, who had learned that three victims were to be given up to them, he was received with cheers. Further on his progress, however, where the Council's decision had not reached the mob, he had a different reception. His coach was stopped and beset by a crowd who demanded to know what had been done with 'these murderers'. On a volley of stones being thrown from a distance, he stepped from his coach, and the crowd, impressed by his unconcerned demeanour, opened a passage for him to a friend's house which was conveniently near. The day's proceedings closed with the execution of Green and his two companions on the Links of Leith amid the jeers of the exulting populace; and it is on record that they met their fate like brave men, declaring their innocence to the last.[1]

III

On June 28, 1705, the Scottish Parliament met in its third and penultimate session. It was the same Parliament, but the Ministry was different and the distribution of parties was different. The events of

---

[1] Ib., f. 154. They were hanged at Leith because the crime with which they were charged was committed at sea.

the past year had intensified rather than diminished their divisions. It might have been expected that, in view of the attitude of England as announced in the Alien Act, all parties except the ultra-Jacobites would unite in a common policy in the interest of their country. So we may think after the event. But in the existing circumstances it was possible for honest men and good patriots to differ as to what the best policy for their country was. There were two diffi- culties that had to be faced. What was the best arrangement to be made with England in the perma- nent interest of Scotland, and what was the arrange- ment that would most probably commend itself to the Estates? On both of these questions there was honest difference of opinion, and, considering the issues at stake, it was inevitable that the best and the worst passions should have their full course. In the volumi- nous correspondence of the leaders of the different parties we find something to reprobate, but also much that is to the credit of human nature. We have place- hunting and wire-pulling, private interests over-riding public; but in none of the leaders do we miss an anxious concern for the national wellbeing. They mutually revile each other according to the wont of rival politicians. Johnstone calls Seafield 'the greatest villain in the world'; yet we cannot read Seafield's correspondence without seeing that he also gives both his heart and mind to the best counsel for his country.

But to follow the proceedings of the session—the session in which the first step was taken towards the complete union of the two kingdoms—we must have before us both the character of the new Ministry and the state of parties as they now stood. To understand

the readjustments that had taken place, we have to go
back to the close of the preceding session in August,
1704.   During that session the Marquis of Tweeddale
had represented the queen as Royal Commissioner.
With the support of a small following, designated the
New Party, which he had detached from the old
Country Party, he had undertaken to carry an Act of
Succession settling the crown on the House of Hanover.   He had signally failed to accomplish his under-
taking, and it might have been expected that his failure
would at once discredit himself and his party in the
eyes of the queen and her English advisers.   So far
was this from being the case, however, that at the
close of the session the Scottish administration was
virtually put in the hands of the New Party.   Tweeddale was made Chancellor, Seafield and Roxburgh
the two Secretaries of State, Baillie of Jerviswoode
Treasurer-depute ; and other leaders of the same party
were put in the different offices of state.   According
to Lockhart, the favour thus shown to the New Party
was due to the fact that Godolphin regarded them as
the staunchest supporters of his own pet scheme for
solving the difficulties between the two kingdoms—the
settlement of the Scottish crown on Hanover.

But before the New Party had been long in power
it was brought home to Godolphin that as an instrument to effect his ends it was impossible.   Their
conduct of affairs, indeed, had been such as to alienate
all parties in Scotland, and at the same time to embroil
them with England.   It was they who were mainly
responsible for all the trouble that had arisen over the
affair of Captain Green and his crew.   As they saw
the ground slipping from beneath their feet, they made

desperate endeavours to come to terms with the leaders of the Revolution Whigs, and their cipher correspondence, which has been preserved, is the most discreditable of the period.[1] By the beginning of 1705 they began to see that their game was played out. On January 9, Johnstone wrote to Baillie of Jerviswoode: 'Marlborough, you know, will be gone, and Godolphin does all, who, I fear, will abandon you for the Whigs for his own ease, or accept of any offers of undertakers the Whigs will recommend, though no doubt the inclination is for Tweeddale.'

Within two months Johnstone's fears for his party were realized. Godolphin was forced to throw himself, however loth, on the Revolution Whigs—the one party, as the whole course of the reign proved, on which the stability of the existing *régime* depended. In the beginning of April it became known that another Royal Commissioner was to take the place of Tweeddale, the appointment of whom must involve a transformation of the Ministry. He was John, second Duke of Argyle, a youth in his twenty-fifth year. But, in spite of his youth, there were cogent reasons for Godolphin's selection of him for the most prominent position that could be held by a Scotsman. He was the representative of a family canonized in Presbyterian memories. Two of his ancestors had been executed for their opposition to two Stewart kings, and he was himself identified with Presbyterian interests. If any one, therefore, was likely to rally the Whigs to the Government measures, it was he. And he had other family advantages which, just at this period, might count for much. All through the spring and summer

---

[1] Baillie, *Correspondence*, p. 34.

of 1705 there were rumours of a Highland rising in
concert with a French invasion, and Argyle was a
Highland chief who could put 6,000 men in the field,
that is to say, twice as numerous a body as all the
regular forces in the country. But besides these family
recommendations, he had gifts and graces of his own
which, in the estimation of his contemporaries, made
him a notable personality. Noble and distinguished in
manner and appearance, he possessed talents for both
peace and war. His beguiling charm as a speaker is
described by the most critical of judges, Lord Chesterfield. 'The late Duke of Argyle,' Chesterfield says,
'though the weakest reasoner, was the most pleasing
speaker I ever heard in my life. He charmed, he
warmed, he forcibly ravished the audience, not by his
matter certainly, but by his manner of delivering it.
A most genteel figure, a graceful, noble air, an har-
monious voice, an elegancy of style and a strength of
emphasis, conspired to make him the most affecting,
persuasive, and applauded speaker I ever saw.' For
military command, also, he had natural aptitudes, as
his subsequent career was to show. Under Marlborough, and as an independent commander, he so
greatly distinguished himself that he was accounted
the third of British generals. Yet with all his gifts he
was not fitted to lead a political party. To his honour
and probity, indeed, Lockhart bears high testimony :
'his word [was] so sacred that one might assuredly
depend upon it.' But his temper was imperious and
violent, and, as both Chesterfield and Lockhart have
noted, he was lacking in the more solid qualities of
a statesman. It was his characteristic threat that he
would run through the body any satirist who made

free with his name that elicited the well-known couplet of Pope —

Argyle, the State's whole thunder born to wield,
And shake alike the senate and the field.

In Argyle it will be seen that Anne and her minister Godolphin had another personage to deal with than the suave Queensberry and the vacillating Tweeddale. The story of his acceptance of the Commissionership is told in his correspondence recently published, and what emerges from the correspondence is that he would accept office only on his own terms. There were two questions that had to be settled before the Estates met. Was the New Party to be cashiered or not? This was the first question. The second was, what measures should be submitted to the Estates as most likely to establish better relations between the two nations? What is singular is, that neither of these two all-important questions was determined before Argyle's going to Scotland. He had given it clearly to be understood that he would accept office only on condition that the New Party should be dismissed, but Godolphin refused to commit himself. And we can understand his perplexity. As has already been said, it was his policy to keep in touch with the leaders of all parties, and advices which he now received led him to hesitate as to the prudence of following Argyle's counsel. Above all, he was assured by Seafield that only a union of the old and the new parties could ensure the passing of royal measures in the approaching session. We see Godolphin's dilemma. He could not afford to throw over Argyle, and yet he doubted the wisdom of Argyle's policy. The final arrangement was that, on Argyle's arrival in Scotland, the queen would intimate her decision.[1]

Argyle came down to Scotland in the first week of April, and on May 6 he wrote to Godolphin that he had taken counsel with all her Majesty's servants whom he could trust, and found them unanimous that the New Party must go and that the Government must be 'all of a piece', if her Majesty's measures were to be carried. Even yet Godolphin was unable to make up his mind, and Argyle wrote to the queen offering his resignation. The meeting of the Estates was at hand, and some decision was imperative. In the last week of May Argyle was told that his terms were accepted and that he was at liberty to form such a Ministry as he thought desirable. The dismissal of the New Party immediately followed, and their places were filled by a Ministry almost exclusively Whig.[2] The Earls of Loudoun and Annandale were made Secretaries, the Earl of Glasgow Treasurer-Depute, Queensberry Lord Privy Seal, and Seafield retained his office of Chancellor. Of all these men Seafield alone was not an undiluted Whig, and he had been retained as a useful intermediary between the various parties.

The Ministry thus formed, the next question was what measure was most likely to be approved by the majority of the House. On this question there was no

[1] *Intimate Society Letters of the Eighteenth Century*, edited by the Duke of Argyll, Lond., 1910, pp. 15–17.

[2] From Argyle's letters we learn that he had a personal ambition that may have had some influence on his conduct. He was desirous of an English peerage, which Anne promised him and subsequently granted. Seafield states that it was the promise of the peerage that determined him to accept the Commissionership.—*Seafield Letters*, Add. MSS. Brit. Mus. 28055, f. 196.

such unanimity as in the case of the formation of the Ministry, and the conflicting opinions are a remarkable commentary on the cross-currents that intersected all parties. There were but two measures, Argyle told Godolphin, that were in the option of her Majesty : the one was the settlement of the succession, the other a treaty. Of the two, the first was the more desirable ; the second the more likely to pass. This was Argyle's opinion, but it was not shared by the majority of his colleagues. At a meeting expressly called to settle the point, six Ministers were in favour of a treaty, and two in favour of the succession. In this dilemma there was only one course open. Two drafts of a royal letter were prepared, in one of which the Union was put first, and in the other the Succession—the responsibility of the choice being left with the queen and her advisers. When the authorized royal letter at length came, it was found that the precedence had been given to the succession. By this decision the continuity of the royal policy was at least maintained, as the passing of a Succession Act had been the chief charge to Tweeddale as Commissioner in the preceding session. Warned by the miscarriage of the succession in the previous year, however, the royal letter suggested an alternative : if it was found that an Act of Succession could not be carried, the attempt should be made to pass an act for a Treaty of Union.

IV

Before the session began Argyle informed Godolphin that he did not hold himself responsible for the success of her Majesty's measures, and that it was only with this proviso that he retained his office. Godolphin had delayed so long before consenting to dismiss the New Party that he must abide by the consequences.[1] Argyle had good reasons for his uncertainty, as a glance at the parties in the House, as they were now arrayed, will show. And be it said that they now assumed the form which they were to retain till the House abolished itself as a legislative body. There was the permanent Court Party on which the Ministers could generally depend for supporting their measures, but which, as they knew, did not constitute a majority in the House. 'I am sure we have not a majority to carry everything,'[2] Seafield wrote to Godolphin, and it was in view of this fact that he had recommended the retention of the New Party. Moreover, the Ministers themselves were not all of one mind. To the indignation of Argyle, the Marquis of Annandale, one of the two Secretaries of State,[3] insisted on taking a way of his own, and refused to support the most important measure of the session, with the result that he was eventually dismissed from office.[4] In these circumstances the only hope for the government was to win such supporters from the other parties as might be of wavering convictions or were open to Court influence. And Argyle, like previous Commissioners, had been supplied with the means of persuasion. He was empowered to grant six knighthoods and four Green Ribbons to such persons as he thought deserving

---

[1] *Intimate Society Letters*, pp. 18, 19.

[2] *Seafield Letters*, Add. MSS. Brit. Mus. 28055, f. 246.

[3] The arrangement between the two Secretaries was that they should act in alternate months.

[4] See App. III. Letters of Annandale.

of these honours, and to be as liberal with pensions as
funds would allow. The second party was that of the
Jacobites, who, as in previous sessions, embarrassed
the government by all the tactics their ingenuity could
devise. Their leader was the Duke of Hamilton, who,
however, according to Lockhart, showed 'less zeal and
forwardness' than in former sessions,[1] and who, as we
shall see, was to astonish his followers by one of those
unexpected actions which puzzled his contemporaries.
The third section in the House was that New Party
whose leaders had been removed from the Ministry
before the session began. It now, however, begins to
be more commonly designated by another name. In
view of the policy it followed of attaching itself now
to one party and now to another, it was called the
'Squadrone Volante'[2]—a designation possibly suggested by Fletcher, who was a student of Italian. Its
most prominent member calls for a passing notice,
since, as already said, he had still a great part to play
in the future. He was John, fifth Earl of Roxburgh,
and was now only about twenty-five years of age. By
his contemporaries of all shades of opinion he was
regarded as a paragon of graces and accomplishments.
Lockhart, in whose eyes he was 'the very bane and
cut-throat of his country', says of him that he was
perhaps 'the best-accomplished young man of quality
in Europe, and had so charming a way of expressing
his thoughts that he pleased even those against whom
he spoke'. Both in the present session and in the
momentous one that was to follow, the Squadrone,

---

[1] Lockhart, *Memoirs*, p. 115.

[2] The designation had been applied at an earlier date, but its use
now becomes more common in the documents of the time.

which now could reckon sixteen[1] votes and counted two other nobles among its leaders—the Marquis of Tweeddale, the late Commissioner, and the Marquis of Montrose—frequently swayed the balance between the regular opposition and the government.

But the man on whom the Ministry had most to depend for the success of its measures was the Duke of Queensberry, who had been under a cloud as the result of the Plot associated with his name. As we have seen, he had played a mischievous part in the previous session by allying himself with the Jacobites against the government. Since then, however, he had changed his tactics and, in close association with Argyle, was now working in the interests of his former friends, the Revolution Whigs. He did not appear at the beginning of the session, on account of the state of his health, he himself gave out; according to Lockhart, for fear of the question of the Plot being raised. His coming was anxiously awaited both by Argyle and Seafield—and for good reasons, since during his absence his following systematically voted against the government. When he did appear, his adroitness and his influence with his party decisively turned the scale in favour of the Ministry and enabled them to carry the all-important measure of the session.[2] It was for these services that in the following session he was chosen Commissioner, as of all his countrymen most likely to carry the Treaty of Union to a successful conclusion.

[1] Authorities differ as to the number ; possibly because it varied.

[2] ' The Duke of Queensberry was mighty diligent in this measure and did effectually prevail with many of his friends.'—Seafield to Godolphin, Add. MSS. Brit. Mus. 28055, f. 265.

Be it remembered that, when the session began, the
menace of the Alien Act was hanging over the country.
The House met at the close of June, and on the 25th
of the following December the act would come into
operation. From that date England would treat
Scotsmen as aliens, and the most lucrative Scotch
commodities would be prohibited from passing the
Border. There can be no doubt that the disastrous
consequences that would follow the act were a present
consideration in the minds of the members of all
parties, yet the opposition showed itself as little conciliatory to England as in the previous two sessions.
'In short,' wrote Godolphin to Seafield, 'it looks to me
as if that nation desired to bring things to extremity,
in which I am not sure they are very well advised.'[1]
It would be unjust, however, to charge the whole body
of the opposition with mere blind prejudice or irre-
sponsible hostility to England. There were issues at
stake which involved both principles and convictions
regarding which there was room for the most diverse
opinions. We have seen the general ground on which
the successive Ministries had been so persistently
opposed—the fixed suspicion that they were unduly
influenced by English Ministers in English interests;
and that there were good reasons for the suspicion the
documents of the time leave us in no doubt. On the
two royal measures that were to be laid before the
House—that for settling the succession and that for
nominating Commissioners to treat of Union—the
shrewdest observers might well disagree regarding
their possible results for the country. For the Presbyterian Whigs the settlement of the succession on the

[1] *Hist. MSS. Com., Fourteenth Report* App , Part III, p. 207.

House of Hanover would be the seal and assurance
that Protestantism would be permanently safeguarded.
Jacobites, like Lockhart, on the other hand, regarded
such a settlement as the death-knell of their hopes,
while others, like Fletcher, saw in it no security for
better treatment from England than in the past. So
also with regard to a Treaty of Union. Men like
Argyle and Seafield and Queensberry were convinced
that only by means of a Treaty could the common
interests of the two kingdoms be satisfactorily adjusted;
while others, like Hamilton and Atholl, were equally
convinced that, in view of the relative resources of
the negotiating parties, a Treaty would involve the
surrender of independent national existence.

The session had not well begun before the Ministers
found that the measure to which the royal letter had
given precedence—the settling of the succession—
had as little chance of passing as in the previous year.
The other string to their bow was the measure for
appointing Commissioners of Union, and to the carrying of this measure all their energies were given during
the remainder of the session. It was an uphill fight
from the beginning, as the opposition made play with
every means of obstruction at their disposal. The
person who had the distinction of introducing the bill
was John, Earl of Mar, whose subsequent career as
the equivocal hero of the Rising of the 'Fifteen was to
be a singular commentary on his present action. The
bill was introduced on July 20, but it was not till the last
week of August that it came up for serious consideration.
The line taken by the opposition was that it would be
ignominious to offer to treat with a nation which had
outraged Scottish feeling by the Alien Act. If an

offer to treat were made, it should be on the one condition that that act should first be rescinded by the
Parliament of England. To have a clause to that
effect inserted in the bill, therefore, was the opposition's
strenuous endeavour. The insertion of such a clause,
they anticipated, would effectually ruin the prospects
of a treaty, as the English Parliament would naturally
resent a demand, the granting of which would be an
offence to the English people. It was the adroit
Queensberry who rescued the Ministers from their
difficulty. He proposed and carried a resolution to
the effect that, instead of adding the conditional clause
to the bill, the House should direct a special Address
to the queen in which she should be told of its
resentment against the high-handed action of her
English Parliament.

An all-important question still remained to be settled.
Who was to appoint the Commissioners whose business
it would be to negotiate a Treaty? In his private
instructions Argyle had received stringent orders to
secure their nomination by the queen. There was
a final and bitter contest on a point on which, in truth,
depended the prospect of successful negotiation. Commissioners appointed by the queen, it was contended,
would be persons certain to be unduly under English
influence. The Government found an unexpected
ally. At a late hour, after a prolonged sitting of the
House, the Duke of Hamilton rose, addressed the
Chancellor, and moved that the nomination of the
Commissioners should be left to the queen. It was
the most dramatic incident of the session. As Lockhart describes the scene, the Jacobites were thunder-
struck by the duke's action; and 'about twelve or

fifteen of them ran out of the House in rage and
despair'. By this ill-advised action, he adds, the
Government found its opportunity, and Hamilton's
motion was carried by a majority of eight.[1]

'From this day', is Lockhart's comment, 'we date
the commencement of Scotland's ruin,'—words which
in his language meant that union was now inevitable.
But this was an opinion based on later events, and
was so far from being general at the time when the
act for union was passed, that he was nearer the truth
when he says elsewhere that neither at that time nor
much later was there a man in Britain who expected
it.[2] In point of fact, many members of the House
who voted for the act had no sincere desire for union.
In the intention of some it was a tactical stroke which
further postponed the passing of an Act of Succession.
Others supported it because it seemed 'a remote thing',
which in the end must prove abortive. As events were
to prove, hostility to union was not confined to the
Estates : it was shared by the great majority of the
Scottish people. Nor in England did the prospect of
union appear more promising; in the opinion of both
nations, is the remark of Bishop Burnet, union was
'a chimaera of the English Ministry',[3] and he expressed
the conviction of some of the shrewdest of his contemporaries.

[1] Lockhart, *Memoirs*, i, pp. 132–3 : Hume of Crossrig says that the
majority was 'about 40'.—*Op. cit.*, p. 171 : In a letter to Godolphin
Seafield suggests an explanation of Hamilton's action : he was
desirous of a place in the government.—*Seafield Letters*, f. 196.

[2] Lockhart, *op. cit.*, i. 133, 140.

[3] Burnet, *History of his Own Time*, Oxford, 1823, v. 221.

LECTURE V

THE TREATY OF UNION

I

THE act appointing Scots Commissioners to treat of union received the royal sanction on September 28th, 1705. Both nations now saw that they were face to face with a crisis in their destinies. In Scotland it was the general conviction that, if the negotiations miscarried, the result must be civil war. In words already quoted, the Earl of Roxburgh expressed this conviction : ' I am throughly convinc'd that, if we do not go into the Succession or an Union very soon, conquest will certainly be upon the first peace.' From the close of the parliamentary session of 1705, therefore, the all-absorbing concern of Scottish statesmen and the Scottish nation was the probable success or failure of the impending negotiations.

There was a possibility, indeed, that negotiations might never take place. In their Address to the Queen, the Estates had given her to understand that, unless the Alien Act were previously repealed, the Scottish Commissioners would engage in no negotiation for a treaty. It was the hope of the majority who insisted on this condition that the English Parliament would refuse to rescind its act, and thus foreclose all negotiations. But it seemed that events were working in favour of a mutual understanding between the two peoples. By an auspicious coincidence, only about a month after the Scottish Estates rose, a new English Parliament met (October 25). It was a predominantly Whig Parliament, and union was essentially a Whig policy, since only by union could the Revolution Settlement be permanently safeguarded. From the beginning, therefore, the attitude of both Houses to Scottish affairs was eminently conciliatory. The queen in her speech earnestly recommended union in the best interests of both kingdoms ; and Lords and Commons, Whigs and Tories consenting, unanimously agreed to repeal the objectionable act—the clause excluding Scots commodities from England as well as the Alien clause. This was of good omen for the spirit in which negotiations would be undertaken, and as such it was regarded by the Scottish Ministry. 'The English frankness in this affair,' wrote the Earl of Mar, now one of the Secretaries of State, 'by doing more than we ourselves proposed, I think should make people in Scotland in good humour.'[1] Still more emphatic in his appreciation of what the English concession imported was another Scottish statesman of weightier metal than Mar, the Earl of Stair. 'I am well convinced', Stair wrote, 'the English have done very handsomely and obligingly in repealing all the clauses of their act which were either injurious or grievous to us ; and, though there were no more success to be hoped for from the same treaty, yet that same was well worth all the struggle we had to obtain it.'[2]

---

[1] *Carstares State Papers*, p. 739.

[2] J. M. Graham, *Stair Annals* (1875), i. 210

II

The course now cleared for negotiations, Scottish statesmen of all shades of opinion had to face the prospect of a treaty, whether they liked it or not. There are two streams of correspondence that reveal the respective attitudes of the leaders of the different parties. We have the correspondence of those not in the government, notably that of the Squadrone Volante; and that of the government officials, specially of Seafield and Mar—the one Lord Chancellor, the other, as has been said, one of the two Secretaries of State.

The inter-communications of the leaders of the Squadrone are contained in the Correspondence of George Baillie of Jerviswoode. Baillie has already been named as a prominent member of his party, but, in view of the part he was to play, he calls for more special mention. According to Lockhart, he was 'by far the most significant man of all his party, to whom he was a kind of dictator', and the deference paid to him by his various correspondents bears out Lockhart's statement. He had identified himself with the Revolution from the first, and was in favour of the Hanoverian succession, the settlement of which he considered preferable to union. When union came to hold the field, however, he gave it his hesitating support as the only means of averting civil war. Though 'of a profound solid judgment', he did not possess the oratorical gifts and graces of the other Squadrone leader, the Earl of Roxburgh, who was, therefore, more conspicuous in the public eye.

The correspondence of the leaders of the Squadrone

—Baillie, Roxburgh, and Johnstone—is not pleasant reading. It is the revelation of the machinations of a party bent on maintaining its separate existence and taking advantage of every turn in the development of events. On the whole, they were disposed to favour union, though all their followers were not similarly minded. ' If they design to settle this countrey upon a good foot, it's well,' Baillie writes, ' we must be partakers of the glorie and advantage, seeing they cannot succeed without us '. 'After all,' he writes on another occasion, ' considering the temper of this people, how unfit to govern themselves . . . I must be convinced that union is our onlie game.' Roxburgh was equally clear in the same conviction : ' the more I think of union ', he says, ' the more I like it, seeing no security anywhere else ', but, he significantly adds, he will take care to keep his mind to himself.[1] The explanation of Roxburgh's reticence appears in a letter of Baillie. ' To oppose good things, or to set up our enemies, are equally hard. One of them will be our case : but what remedie ? ' The Squadrone, it will be seen, was playing a waiting game, and they played it so well that till the opening of the session of the Parliament that was to decide the fate of the treaty, no one knew on what side their vote would be cast, though the general impression was that it would not be cast for union.[2] As in the end was proved, they did give their support to the treaty, and they claimed that only by their support could it have been passed, seeing they held the balance of the House in their hands.[3]

[1] Baillie, *Correspondence*, pp. 134, 141, 145.
[2] Lockhart, *Memoirs*, i. 159.
[3] But see below, p. 122.

With their own convictions, indeed, they could not have acted otherwise, if Roxburgh spoke the mind of his party when he said that, if the Union failed, the Pretender must come in.[1]

We turn to the correspondence of the government officials during the same period and find them pre-occupied with two main concerns. The one was to gain supporters for the treaty; the other to ensure such a body of Commissioners as would give it the best chance of success. The two men whose influence they were most anxious to secure were the Marquis of Annandale and the Duke of Argyle. We have heard of Argyle's quarrel with Annandale, whose dismissal from the Secretaryship as an impossible colleague he persistently demanded. He was actually dismissed, but the government felt that they could not afford to lose him, and he was offered the post of Lord Privy Seal which he had previously held. Though the queen herself made a special appeal to him, however, Annandale refused the offer, and even made overtures to the Squadrone, which were coldly received. To the end he was an obdurate enemy of the Treaty of Union in all its stages, yet Lockhart's charge that his opposition was due to his removal from office is probably unjust. From his correspondence it appears that before his dismissal he had the fixed conviction that the settlement of the succession was a preferable measure to a treaty.[2]

Argyle, the Ministers knew, was indispensable to the success of the treaty, yet at one moment it seemed as if they were to lose him. As Commissioner during

[1] Baillie, *Correspondence*, p. 138.
[2] See Appendix III.

the late session, indeed, he had used all his influence to carry the act for the appointment of Commissioners for union. In the spring of 1706, however, he had gone to the Low Countries to win military laurels under Marlborough, and it was while he was in this service that the difficulty with him arose. Argyle always had a due sense of his own importance, and was not disposed to give his services for naught. While Commissioner, he had let it be known that he must have an English peerage. Now he intimated that he must have the commission of a major-general, but Marlborough, who had no love for him, was reluctant. It was while he was nursing his chagrin that he received a letter from Godolphin urging him to return and give his support to the Union. This is how he comments to Mar on Godolphin's communication, and the passage is so characteristic that it deserves to be quoted. 'My Lord, it is surprising to me that my Lord Treasurer [Godolphin], who is a man of sense, should think of sending me up and down like a footman from one country to another without ever offering me any reward. There is indeed a certain service due from every subject to his prince, and that I shall pay the Queen as faithfully as anybody can do; but if her Ministers think it for her service to employ me any further, I do think the proposal should be attended with the offer of a reward. . . . My Lord, when I have justice done me here and am told what to expect for going to Scotland, I shall be ready to obey my Lord Treasurer's commands.'[1] Marlborough, who was as convinced as Godolphin of the necessity of union, saw

[1] *Papers of the Earl of Mar and Kellie*, Hist. MSS. Com. (1904), p. 270.

fit to strike the bargain ; Argyle received his commission as major-general, and returned to Scotland in
time to give his support to the articles of the treaty
when under consideration of the Estates. As Mar
afterwards avouched that the passing of the treaty was
due to Argyle above all others, the commission was
well bestowed.[1]

The other concern of the Scottish Ministers was the
choice of the Commissioners to be entrusted with the
negotiation of the treaty. On their choice must
absolutely depend any prospects of its success. There
were two opinions regarding the principles on which
they should be selected. Some, like the aged Earl of
Marchmont, held that the main body of them should
be 'sound and well inclined' to union, but that those
opposed to union should be represented by their most
influential leaders, who would thus have the opportunity
of raising objections to the Treaty before it reached
the Estates.[2] Others were of opinion that the only
method of ensuring success was to select the Commissioners exclusively from known supporters of the
government.[3] The ultimate decision lay with one
man—the Duke of Queensberry. By his services in
the late session Queensberry had made himself the
most important person in the country. It was mainly
owing to his adroitness and his personal influence that
the act for appointing a Commission had been carried
in the teeth of all opposition, and he was already
marked as the one man who was most likely to ensure
the success of the Treaty. In coming to his decision

---

[1] Mar contradicts himself on this point.
[2] *Marchmont Papers*, iii, pp. 288, 293, 299.
[3] *Mar and Kellie Papers*, p. 242.

he had the counsel of one who bears a sinister name in the memories of his countrymen—John, first Earl of Stair, the prime agent in the proceedings that resulted in the Massacre of Glencoe. Stair had taken a prominent part in Parliamentary debate since the beginning of the reign, but it was in the final session and in connexion with the Union that he was to give full display of his remarkable powers. According to De Foe, he was 'the man of greatest counsel in the kingdom'; according to Lockhart, 'there was none in the Parliament capable to take up the cudgels with him'. Stair was himself convinced of the necessity of an incorporating union, but he deprecated overhaste in pressing it. The wiser policy, he thought, was to settle matters of trade first, then the succession, and union would follow in due course.[1]

In concert with Stair and other government leaders, Queensberry, in the beginning of December, drew up a memorial in which were set forth the principles on which the Commissioners were to be chosen. This memorial, together with a suggested list, was forwarded to Mar, who was instructed to submit it to the queen.[2] How far this original list was modified we do not know, as it was after consultations between Queensberry and Godolphin that the nominations were finally made on February 27, 1706.[3] One fact reveals the principles on which the nominations were made: of the thirty-one Commissioners only three voted against the Treaty of Union when it came before the Estates. All the

---

[1] *Mar and Kellie Papers*, p. 243.

[2] *Ib.*, p. 240. Argyle is not mentioned as being present.

[3] Queensberry appears to have insisted, under the threat of resignation, that the list should not be much altered.

Ministers, except one, were nominees, and the three
Estates—the nobles, smaller barons, and burghers—
were all represented. The leaders of the Squadrone,
who had been in doubt if they should accept nomination if it were offered, were left out. Argyle, who was
offended at the omission of Hamilton, to whom he had
come under a pledge, declined to act. On the other
hand, the Jacobite Lockhart accepted nomination,
salving his political conscience by the consideration
that he would have the opportunity of seeing the
enemy's hands. About a fortnight later (April 10) the
English Commission was nominated—a less delicate
matter. It consisted mainly of Whig Lords, the two
Archbishops, and legal officials. The two most influential men on their respective sides were the Lord Chancellor Seafield and Lord Somers, the latter of whom
was the inspiring and guiding spirit throughout the
negotiations.

The two Commissions met on April 16, 1706, in
the Cockpit at Whitehall. Discreetly chosen as they
had been, there was a fair probability that their negotiations would be attended with success. Moreover, the
points that would come up for discussion were known
beforehand, and had frequently been the subject of
consideration. Yet every precaution was taken to
preclude the possibility of friction from the collision of
tempers. Four preliminary articles determined the
manner in which business was to be conducted : every
proposal coming from either Commission and every
conclusion adopted was to be reduced to writing ; no
finding was to be held obligatory till all the articles
assumed their final form ; a Committee from each was
to revise the minutes, subject to the approval of both

Commissions; and, finally, all the proceedings were to
be kept secret during the time of the negotiations.[1]
An unwritten rule, the prudence of which we can
understand, is another illustration of the serious spirit
in which the two Commissions regarded their task:
throughout the whole of their proceedings there was
no interchange of hospitality. 'None of the English
during the Treaty had one of the Scots so much as to
dine or drink a glass of wine with him.'[2]

At the second meeting of the Commissions the
foundations of a Treaty of Union were solidly laid.
At that meeting Cowper, the Lord Keeper, on behalf
of the English Commissioners, submitted these three
proposals: that the two kingdoms should be united
under the name of Great Britain; that the United
Kingdom should be represented by one Parliament;
and that the succession to the crown should devolve
on the House of Hanover in accordance with the
English Act of Settlement. The Scots Commissioners
were fully prepared for these proposals. More than
a month before the negotiations began, Mar had written
as follows: 'they [the English] tell us plainly they
will give us no terms that are considerable for going
into their succession, if any, without going into an
entire union; and, if we insist upon that, they will
never meet with us; for many think all the notions
about federal unions and forms a mere jest and
chimaera. I write this freely to you, though it is not
fit this should be known in Scotland for fear of dis-
couraging people and making them despair of the
treaty. You see that what we are to treat of is not

[1] *Acts of Parl. of Scot.*, xi, App. p. 165.
[2] *Mar and Kellie Papers*, p. 271.

in our choice, and that we see the inconveniences of treating on incorporating union only.'[1] This letter of Mar throws an interesting light on the situation. England was bent on an incorporating union, while Scotland (and we know the fact from other testimony besides that of Mar) was as strongly in favour of federation. We know also that, like Mar, the majority of the Scots Commissioners would have preferred a federal union, not on the ground of its being the best arrangement, but because it was more likely to receive the sanction of the Estates. Notable, also, is the fact that, before the negotiations began, an incorporating union was understood by the Scots to be an imperative condition of a treaty. Seafield, indeed, submitted three counter-proposals to those of Cowper, which substituted federation[2] for incorporation, but this was a mere form, and was probably intended to suggest that he and his fellow-Commissioners had agreed to incorporation only under compulsion. As it was, the head and front of their offending in the eyes of the mass of their country-men was their consenting to incorporation, which was stigmatized as a betrayal of their country. It was this reproach that the opponents of union employed most successfully in inflaming the passions of the mob, and *treaters traitors* became a byword of the day.

As the controversial points that arose in the subsequent negotiations will afterwards come up for consideration, it is unnecessary to note them at this point. Safeguarded for Scotland by the Treaty, as it came from the hands of the Commissioners, were her

---

[1] *Carstares State Papers*, pp. 743-4.

[2] The model of a federal union in the minds of those who advocated it was that of the Low Countries.

law and Courts of Law, the feudal jurisdictions of the barons, and the privileges of the royal burghs. Religion was excluded from the scope of the Commission, but was subsequently to receive special consideration when the articles of the treaty came to be discussed in the Scottish Parliament. After sitting for nine weeks the Commission rose on the 23rd of July, and the conclusion of its labours was signalized by formalities befitting the importance of the occasion. The garrulous Mar has described them for us. ' You cannot imagine ', he wrote to his brother, ' how agreeable it was to everybody here our concluding the treaty and delivering of it to the Queen, which was done very solemnly. She summoned us to meet at the Council Chamber at St. James. We walked through the rooms from that to the room Her Majesty was in to receive us, where were all the ladies and the Court and the foreign ambassadors. One of us and one of the English walked together, and so on; we on the left hand as we walked, but we were on the Queen's right hand. The Keeper and our Chancellor made a speech when they delivered the books . . . .'[1] With reference to the speeches of Seafield and Cowper, another Scots Commissioner who was present on the occasion has some remarks which a Scot may be pardoned for quoting. Lord Seafield's speech, he says, ' excelled the other so far that it was spoken without hesitation, whereas that of the Lord Keeper was miserably mangled in the delivery, and at last he was forced to draw it out of his pocket and read it. However, as he was a very eloquent man and a great lawyer, he was so conscious of his own merit that he never changed colour at his

[1] *Mar and Kellie Papers*, p. 271.

accident, but first stopped a little, and then read his paper with great composure of mind, while all the audience was in the utmost pain for him'.[1]

III

The terms of a Treaty of Union being now settled, it remained to be seen how they would be received by the Parliaments of the two kingdoms. It was arranged that they should be first submitted to the Parliament of Scotland, as they were likely to meet with most opposition in that body. It was with no assured confidence that the Scottish Ministers looked forward to the result of its deliberations. In the three previous sessions the government could not command a majority of the House, and it would only be by adroit management of the conflicting elements in the opposition that success could be secured. Moreover, in view of the momentous question that was to be settled, there would be a factor at work which had to be seriously reckoned with. In the case of Captain Green we have seen how public opinion had concussed the Ministry of the day into foolish and criminal action. Since the independent existence of the kingdom was now at stake, would not public opinion assert itself with such vehemence as to paralyse the deliberations of the Estates? Before the session began, the government fully understood that the great majority of those who had control of public opinion were opposed to an incorporating union. By far the most influential persons in directing the opinion of the country at large were

[1] *Memoirs of the Life of Sir John Clerk of Penicuik*, Scot. Hist. Soc. (1892), pp. 62–3.

the national clergy, who, as a body, dreaded an incorporating union as inevitably involving the ruin of the Presbyterian settlement. In the treatment of dissent in England they saw what they might expect from a single Parliament sitting in London, the great majority of whose members were Episcopalians, who would naturally desire to see their own form of church-government established in Scotland. So soon as the purport of the treaty was known, therefore, the pulpits throughout the country rang with denunciations of its authors, and engagements were entered into by the ministers, elders, deacons, and parishioners to resist it to the utmost of their power.[1] Fortunately, as we shall see, there were wiser heads among the national clergy who were able to make such terms with the government as to ensure the permanent safety of their Church.

There were other guides of public opinion who for different reasons were equally opposed to union. The Episcopalian clergy, who had numerous congregations in certain parts of the country, dreaded it for a reason precisely opposite to that for which the Presbyterians dreaded it: their fear was that it would permanently establish Presbyterianism as the national form of church-government. More formidable than the opposition of the Episcopalians was that of another religious body of which something has already been said.[2] These were the Cameronians, who had dissociated themselves from the main body of the Presbyterians for their sinful compliance with the government of Charles II. Since the Revolution they

[1] *Portland MSS.*, Hist. MSS. Com., vol. viii, p. 247.

[2] See above, p. 10.

had been without ministers, but there were leaders
among them who could direct their councils.   In the
eyes of the Cameronians, union with England was an
impious compact with a nation blind to the first principles of the Christian religion.   So irreconcilable was
their attitude that the government had grounds to
fear that they would join hands with the Jacobites in
resisting by open force the passing of the treaty.
Finally, there were influential persons in all parts of
the country who for various reasons were hostile to
union, and who systematically set themselves to inflame
national sentiment with the deliberate purpose of pro-
voking civil war.   Such, for example, was the Duchess
of Hamilton, who industriously used all her influence
to rouse her neighbourhood to open rebellion.   What
came of the action of all these hostile forces we shall
presently see.   With what uncertainty the government
regarded the prospect of the treaty appears from these
words of Mar addressed to Godolphin on the eve of
the meeting of the Estates.   'Upon the whole affair,'
Mar wrote, 'until the Parliament once meet and so the
members be all come here, it is hard to make such
a conjecture that your Lordship can rely on.'[1]

IV

The last Scottish Parliament met in its last session
on October 3rd, 1706.   For the third time since the
beginning of the reign the Duke of Queensberry
represented the queen, as by the unanimous opinion
of those who favoured a Treaty of Union he was the
one man who had any chance of piloting it successfully

[1] *Mar and Kellie Papers*, p. 278.

in the face of the opposition it was likely to meet. As in the case of previous Royal Commissioners, he received certain private instructions beyond which he was not to go. His prime business was to do his utmost to carry the twenty-five Articles of the treaty with as little alteration as possible; if any alterations were found necessary, they were to be submitted to the queen. If he found that the majority of the House were opposed to an incorporating union, the Parliament was to be adjourned. Proposals for a federal union, or for settling the succession with limitations, were to be rejected. The settlement of the Church was to be left to the House on the condition that nothing in the settlement should prevent the Parliament of Great Britain from granting such toleration to Dissenters in Scotland as was granted to Dissenters in England.[1] From these instructions it will appear to what extent Scotland managed her own affairs previous to the Union. In one pointed sentence Johnstone put her position before Marlborough, who entirely agreed with him. 'As for the giving up the legislative,' he said, 'he (Marlborough) knew we had none to give up, for the true state of the matter was, whether Scotland should continue subject to an English Ministry without [the privilege] of trade or to be subject to an English Parliament with [the privilege] of trade.'[2]

The leading spokesmen in the new session were the same as in the preceding ones. The champions of the Ministry were the Lord Chancellor Seafield and the Earl of Stair; Hamilton, Atholl, and Annandale headed

---

[1] *Warrant Books of Scotland*, Record Office, London, vol. xxii, nos. 32, 33, 36.

[2] Baillie, *Correspondence*, pp. 176–7.

the Opposition; and the Earls of Marchmont and Roxburgh led the Squadrone. Lockhart and Fletcher, both from their different points of view in desperation at the prospect of their country's ruin, were as indefatigable as ever in their endeavours to thwart the government. Two other members of the House, who have not hitherto been noticed, also call for mention. The name of one of them, Lord Belhaven, is writ large in the history of the dying months of the Scottish Parliament. He is described as a 'rough, fat, black, noisy man, more like a butcher than a lord ',[1] but, like almost every other Scots noble of the time, he was widely read and accomplished. There was no bitterer opponent of union than Belhaven,[2] and his melodramatic rhetoric, which occasionally moved the laughter of the House, was well calculated to inflame national sentiment out of doors. A passage in one of his published speeches (for he was careful to publish them) is familiar to the reader of Scottish history. 'I think I see our ancient mother Caledonia, like Caesar, sitting in the midst of our senate, ruefully looking round about her, covering herself with her royal garment, and breathing out her last with an *Et tu, mi fili.*' And the reply of the Earl of Marchmont is equally well known: 'Behold he dreamed, but lo! when he awoke, he found it was a dream.' Very different in his style of oratory was Seton of Pitmedden, one of the ablest supporters of

---

[1] Macky, *Memoirs*, p. 236.

[2] Belhaven's opposition to the Union may not uncharitably be explained by his being turned out of office. In a letter addressed to Seafield (February 24, 1705) we find him asking for ' a new mark of her [Majesty's] favour', which was not granted.—*Seafield Correspondence* (Scot. Hist. Soc.), p. 385.

union. Measured, compact, and logical, his contributions to debate were at once full of matter and inspired by a grave sense of the national issues at stake.[1] Whether, indeed, we look to one side or the other in the great controversy, we cannot but be struck by the fact that there has seldom met in any national crisis a body of men more capable, by talent, by accomplishment, by experience, of grasping the import of the momentous question they had to determine.

A dominating fact of the situation was that throughout the greater part of the session the Ministers were in an enemy's camp. Before the session began the country had been in a state of comparative indifference,[2] and, if the mass of the people had been left to themselves, in this state they would probably have remained. The Parliament had hardly met, however, before there were ominous signs of a change in the public mind. The causes of this change have already been indicated. In many parts of the country, but especially in the western shires, the ministers raised the cry of the Church in danger, and directly incited their parishioners to armed rising in its defence. In town and country agents of the Opposition appealed to national sentiment and to material interests. Union, they declaimed, meant the loss of national independence and enslavement to England, heavier taxes, and trade at the mercy of English merchants who would only go shares as far as pleased themselves. One result of these propaganda was a stream of addresses to the Parliament from all parts of the country—and all to one purport—the iniquity of an incorporating union.

[1] Seton, like some other members of the House, read his speeches.
[2] Defoe notes this fact.

The Ministers made light of the addresses. They were only fit to make kites of, Argyle said. But the general opposition to the Union took a more serious form. In Edinburgh, always noted for the insubordination of its populace, it was at the risk of their lives that the Ministers went to and fro between Holyrood and the Parliament House, and, to the concern of the queen, they were even threatened with assassination. One serious riot made it necessary to quarter troops in the town—an unprecedented occurrence in its history, and it was under their guard that the Ministers made their daily procession. 'I am not very timorous', Mar wrote on November 19, 'and yet I tell you that every day here we are in hazard of our lives.' These manifestations of aversion to union were not confined to Edinburgh. In various parts of the country there were menacing symptoms that rebellion might break out at any moment. In Glasgow, now a town with a population of about 15,000, there was a riot on a scale unprecedented in its history. It was occasioned by the refusal of the magistrates to sign an address against the Union, and by the inflammatory exhortations of the clergy. The mob made themselves masters of the town, and a band of them, headed by one Finlay, marched to Hamilton in the expectation of being joined by other bodies; but their courage gave way on the news of the approach of the royal troops. Of graver menace was a projected plan of action which, if it had been carried out, would inevitably have resulted in civil war. As was originally conceived, the Highland followers of the Duke of Atholl were to join a body of Cameronians, 7,000 strong, march on Edinburgh, 'raise the Parliament', and cut short the proceedings of the legislators. According to Lockhart, the plan miscarried only because the heart of the Duke of Hamilton, one of its promoters, failed him at the last moment. What further disquieted the Ministers was the fact, perfectly well known to them, that Jacobite emissaries were busy at work in the interests of the exiled House. ' In short,' wrote Johnstone to Baillie, 'there are two parties, one at St. Germains, and another at Edinburgh, that have a regular settled correspondence;'[1] and in December it was rumoured that the Pretender was actually in the Highlands and attended by 200 officers.[2] Moreover, in the event of a rising, the royal forces in Scotland at the command of the Ministry were wholly inadequate to deal with it. Such troops as were at their disposal were necessary for the defence of the capital, and on the loyalty of these they could not securely depend. It was at their earnest insistence, therefore, that, as an imperative precaution, English forces were stationed near the Border and in the north of Ireland, and that a contingent from the army in the Low Countries should be in readiness to embark for Scotland should its services be required. ' God knows', was Hamilton's remark on these precautions, ' God knows if that looks like an agreeable union.'[3] It was with well-founded alarm, therefore, that Baillie, a month after the session began, wrote these words to Johnstone, and others expressed themselves to the same purport. ' In short,' Baillie wrote, ' I'm afraid this nation will run into blood,

[1] Baillie, *Correspondence*, p. 177.

[2] *Ib.*, p. 174.

[3] *Portland MSS.*, Hist. MSS. Com., Fourteenth Report, App. III, p. 268.

whether the Union or Succession be settled.'[1] That civil war did not break out, we are assured by more than one authority, was due to one fortuitous circumstance: the severity of the weather and the condition of the roads made locomotion practically impossible.

It was under these conditions that the Ministry had to obtain the sanction of the House to the twenty-five articles of the treaty. The aim of the Opposition was evident from the first days of the session; it was by all the means at their command to force adjournment by persistent and systematic obstruction, an art in which they had become adepts from long practice. Curiously enough, the chief alternative to union which they proposed was the settlement of the succession— the measure they had so decisively rejected in the session of 1704. The objections urged against a Treaty of Union were mainly these: it was contrary to the Claim of Right—the settlement adopted by Scotland at the Revolution; the existing Parliament had received no mandate to deal with a measure which would overthrow the constitution, and it was, therefore, a simple necessity that the constituencies should be consulted and a new House returned; finally, it was in the highest degree imprudent to press a measure to which the country had unmistakably declared itself averse.

As the result proved, a majority of the members were in favour of the principle of union, but two months of the session had gone before the Ministry had full assurance of ultimate success. The manifestations of public hostility to the treaty alarmed many members who were prepared to support the government, and they were, therefore, disposed to

[1] Baillie, *Correspondence*, p. 168.

make alterations in certain of the articles by way of concession to the popular clamour. But, as we have seen, an express charge laid on Queensberry had been that, if alterations were necessary, they should be such as would not be unacceptable to the English Parliament. Fortunately the Ministers were assisted in their efforts by the condition of the main ranks of the Opposition. Its two rival leaders, the Dukes of Hamilton and Atholl, were jealous of each other's influence and acted on no common councils. Regarding the measure of support afforded by the Squadrone contemporary authorities differ. According to Marchmont, who was one of their leaders, they numbered thirty-four in all, and the government could not have carried the treaty without them[1]; according to the Earls of Mar and Leven, both members of the government, they counted only fifteen or sixteen, and their opposition would not have altered the result.[2] On their own principles the Squadrone were bound to support union, but they supported it always with an eye to the interests of their own party. The Squadrone, wrote Baillie of Jerviswoode, their most influential leader, 'has a hard game to act, and possibly the less they act the better.'[3]

The progress of the treaty through the House may be briefly narrated. The Articles were first read and debated in succession, but without being put to the vote. The real struggle began on the 1st of November, about a month after the session began. It was then

[1] *Marchmont Papers*, iii. 328–30.

[2] *Mar and Kellie Papers*, p. 371; *Society Letters*, etc. (ed. Duke of Argyll), p. 53.

[3] Baillie, *Correspondence*, p. 161.

resolved that the successive articles should be voted upon, though on the understanding that they should not receive the sanction of the House till they had all been approved. Three days later the first article, which enacted the union of the two kingdoms, was passed by a majority of thirty-three, and it was in the debate upon this article that Belhaven drew his woful picture of an enslaved Caledonia. On the 5th and 18th of November, the second and third articles, the one devolving the succession on the House of Hanover, and the other enacting that there should be one Parliament for the two kingdoms, were passed by similar majorities. Before the passing of these two articles, however, there intervened an act which the Ministry deemed indispensable to the ultimate success of the treaty. Of all the opponents of union, as we have seen, the Church was the most formidable. 'One thing I must say for the Kirk,' Mar wrote to Godolphin, 'that, if the Union fail, it is owing to them.'[1] The contention of the national clergy was that the Presbyterian settlement made after the Revolution would not be safe under a British Parliament, the overwhelming majority in which would be Episcopalians. It was to allay this fear that there was passed an Act of Security, which declared that the Church as it now existed was 'to continue without any alteration to the people of this land in all succeeding generations'.

The saner of the clergy thus conciliated, the hopes of the government rose, but the battle over most of the remaining articles was long and arduous. Of one day's debate (and there were many such) Mar wrote: 'It grew at last so late and everybody faint

[1] *Mar and Kellie Papers*, p. 315.

with hunger, for most of us had eaten none that day, that a great many grew weary.'[1]   By the opening of the new year (1707) the Ministers began to congratulate themselves that they were now 'in sight of land'.   But there was still a rock ahead from which the treaty was narrowly to escape destruction.   Of all the articles of the treaty the twenty-second, which limited the number of Scottish representatives in the United Parliament to sixty-one, was the most obnoxious.   On the initiation of Hamilton a dramatic stroke was arranged in con-nexion with this article.   The arrangement was that, as an alternative to the treaty, Hamilton was to move the settlement of the succession on the House of Hanover.   As it was known that the Ministers would refuse to consider the alternative, it was agreed that Hamilton should read a protest on the part of the Opposition, who would then in a body leave the House 'not to return again'.   The appointed day came, but Hamilton absented himself, and he was found at home suffering from toothache.   At the urgent instance of his friends he at length appeared, but to the dismay of the Opposition he refused to table the protest.   The opportunity was lost, and the treaty was saved from what might have proved a disastrous blow.   Associated with the passing of the same twenty-second article was a tragic event.   On the day on which it was carried there had been a long and obstinate debate in which the Earl of Stair played his usual prominent part on behalf of the government.   The strain, coming at the close of the prolonged and anxious session, proved too much for his strength, and he died in the course of the

---

[1] *Mar and Kellie Papers*, p. 309.

following night. He has a place among the conspicuous figures of the national history, but posterity has adjudged that the pedestal on which he stands is a 'bad eminence'.

Eight days after the death of Stair, on January 16th, the Commissioner touched the act for Union with the royal sceptre, and, as inviolably bound up with it, the act for the security of the Church. There still remained to be settled a few difficult matters which prolonged the session till the 25th of March. By the fifteenth article of the treaty, as it left the hands of the Commissioners, a sum known as the Equivalent was granted to Scotland as a compensation for becoming a partner in England's debts and for the various losses she had sustained from English trading companies. By those opposed to union, the Equivalent was regarded as a base bribe to the nation. But, the treaty now passed, it devolved on the House to allocate it to the best of its wisdom. Two other points demanded settlement, and, in the case of both, the personal interests of the party leaders occasioned the most violent controversies of the session. The first point raised the question— how were the representative members of the first United Parliament to be elected? Finally, it was resolved, in accordance with the example of the English Parliament now engaged on the treaty, that the representatives should be chosen from the existing House. Still more violent passions were evoked on the second point—the election of peers to sit in the House of Lords. Out of 154 Scottish peers, who were to be the favoured sixteen—the number fixed by the treaty? In the case of the first sixteen, it was decided that the Commissioner should nominate them, but that in the future they should be elected by the peers themselves.

The Ministry had accomplished their task, and few Ministries have carried a great measure in the face of such difficulties. But neither at the time nor for many a day to come did their labours earn the gratitude of the mass of their countrymen. On the contrary, they were denounced as hirelings who had sold their country for English pay. That the charge of venality should be brought against them in an age when venality was found in all high places was a matter of course, and the Jacobite Lockhart specifically made the charge. That pensions and offices were frequently given as inducements to support the measures of the government we have more than once had occasion to note.[1] It should also be noted, however, that there is equally frequent mention of arrears of salaries to Ministers long after they had demitted office. In truth, with the correspondence of the time before us it is difficult to escape the conclusion that the men who were chiefly responsible for carrying the Treaty—Queensberry, Seafield, Argyle, Mar, Roxburgh, Baillie, and the rest —were sincerely convinced that union was the only possible solution of the relations between the two kingdoms, though its immediate results led certain of them subsequently to believe that they had been mistaken. As a sober and deliberate judgement on their proceedings from first to last, the words of Lord Somers, himself above all others responsible for the Treaty of Union, must be received as weighty testimony. On the passing of the act by the Scottish Parliament the Earl of Marchmont sent him a communication in which

[1] See Appendix IV.

he belauded the services of his own party, the Squadrone, and Somers replied as follows: 'I can never
enough commend the firmness and good temper which
the friends of the Union in Scotland have shown from
the first time that affair was brought before Parliament.
. . . It is not possible there should be so great a mistake
in England as to think an affair of so difficult a nature,
and opposed so violently by various interests as the
Union was in Scotland, could have been brought to
a conclusion without a great concurrence of well-
disposed, wise, and dexterous persons, and, therefore,
it would be unjust to ascribe the merit of it to a few.
. . . When we consider the wonderful difficulties of
bringing such a work to pass, we cannot without
astonishment see it brought so far toward a conclusion,
and yet, if a man reflects on the many disadvantages
and dangers both kingdoms lay under while they
continued two, it cannot but seem strange they could
rest so long in a divided state.'[1]

A few words in conclusion regarding the fate of the
treaty in the English Parliament. Its history there
confirms what we know from other evidence—that the
Union was more acceptable to England than to Scotland. Neither in the House of Lords nor in the House
of Commons did the measure meet with serious opposition, though individual members of both Houses
prophesied that it would prove unworkable in practice
and result in bitterer estrangement between the two
nations. Only one addition of importance was made
to the treaty; at the instance of the Spiritual Peers,
an act similar to that which guaranteed the security

[1] *Portland MSS.*, Hist. MSS. Com., Fourteenth Report, App.,
Part III, pp. 158-9.

of the Church of Scotland was added for the safe-guarding of the Church of England. Introduced in the beginning of February, about a fortnight after it had been ratified by the Scottish Estates, the treaty was rapidly passed by large majorities in both Houses, and on March 6 it received the royal assent. The different spirit in which the two Parliaments had done their work was to receive emphatic comment in the years that immediately followed.

LECTURE VI

THREATENED UNDOING OF THE UNION

On the 1st of May, 1707, the day when the Treaty of Union came into force, a correspondent of the Earl of Mar in Edinburgh wrote as follows : ' There is nothing so much taken notice of here to-day as the solemnity in the south part of Britain and the want of it here.' [1] The words are a significant commentary on the different feelings with which the two nations respectively regarded the Union. To England it brought a sense of relief from a dread which had haunted her people from the beginning of the reign. It was the general opinion in England that the Scots were of necessity Jacobite in their sympathies—an opinion to which the unwillingness of the Scottish Parliament to declare for the House of Hanover seemed to give emphatic support. It was Scotland that had given the Stewarts to England, and it was natural that she should be bound to them by ties of pride and affection. It had been an abiding fear of the English people and of English statesmen, therefore, that some day or other a Scottish army, backed by the power of France, would cross the Border in the interest of the exiled House. Twice before, in the reign of Charles I, the Scots had intervened in English affairs with grave consequences,

---

[1] *Papers of the Earl of Mar and Kellie*, p. 389.

and they might play the same game again. By the Treaty of Union, however, Scotland had given its formal sanction to the Hanoverian succession, and thus the menace of her future possible action seemed to be effectually averted. Unmistakable indications showed that England felt a sense of deliverance when the Treaty was an accomplished fact. While the royal assent was being given to it, the guns were fired from the Tower; and the proclamation enjoining a national thanksgiving was joyfully observed by the nation. The two Scotsmen who had been the principal agents in effectuating the Treaty were received with royal honours in their progress south to London. The Commissioner Queensberry was fêted in every town through which he passed, and the nobility and gentry flocked to pay him their respects. As he approached London, 'the whole city turn'd out to meet him'.[1] The Chancellor Seafield was the object of similar enthusiasm. When ten miles from London, he was met by 500 horse and forty coaches, and from the entrance of the city to his lodging he was followed by huzzaing crowds.[2]

Far different was the manner in which the consummation of the Treaty was received in Edinburgh and in Scotland at large. In many parishes the 1st of May was observed as a day of fasting and humiliation. Portents, also, seemed to signify that Scotland's day was over. On the north shores of the Firth of Forth thirty-one whales, from fifteen to twenty-six feet long, were found dead, 'which was very much talkt of as

[1] Sir John Clerk, *Memoirs*, p. 67. Clerk accompanied Queensberry on his progress.

[2] *Seafield Correspondence* (Scot. Hist. Soc.), pp. 431–2.

ominous!'[1] Also of sinister omen was the circumstance that the first tune pealed by the bells of the
church of St. Giles on the fateful morning was: 'Why
should I be sad on my wedding-day?'[2]

It was with these contrasted visions of the future
that the two nations regarded the bond that now united
them. What the statesmen who were responsible for
the knitting of the bond professed to anticipate from
it, we already know. It was the hope of the English
statesmen who had worked for it that Scotland would
cease to be what she had been in the past years of the
reign—a permanent menace to England's security. A
sense of their common interests would gradually unite
the two peoples in common aims; under the influence
of increasing prosperity Jacobitism would die a natural
death; and Scotland would no longer be a 'back-door'
for England's enemies. On their part, the Scottish
statesmen who had advocated union looked for two
direct results from it: it would avert the possibility of
war between the two kingdoms, and place Scotland in
a position more favourable for the development of her
resources. So far as Scotland was concerned, all these
anticipations depended on three contingencies. Would
there be such a manifest increase in the trade and
commerce of the country as to convince the nation
that the Union had been in its best interests? The
great majority of the ministers of the National Church
had been opposed to union, and they were the most
influential body of men in the country. Would they in
time become reconciled to the compact, or, irrecon-

[1] *Papers of the Earl of Mar and Kellie*, p. 389. A printed account
of these whales was sent to Mar.
[2] *Ib.*

cilable: would they use their influence to break it? Finally, what part would national sentiment play under the new conditions? The nation generally had shown itself hostile to the surrender of its independence. Would this hostility grow more intense when the nation was face to face with the subordinate position which necessarily resulted from the extinction of its representative assembly? Let us consider in succession these three contingencies as they were resolved in the remaining years of the reign of Anne. And first as to the hope entertained of increased prosperity in trade and commerce. The details that follow are somewhat tedious, but it is necessary to have them before us if we are to understand the dangers that threatened the Union.

I

It seemed as if a perverse fate attended the first commercial relations of the united kingdoms, and the unhappy start was to have abiding evil consequences. It gave the Scots a bad taste of the Union from the outset, and more than half a century was to pass before they began to have a perception that it might prove a good thing in the end. One misunderstanding followed another, and the conviction became general that England was systematically sacrificing Scotland's interests to her own.

The first cause of friction was perhaps inevitable. By one of the articles of the Union the duties from the Customs and Excise in both countries were to be equalized, and it was arranged that they should be levied in the same manner. In Scotland the arrangement had hitherto been to lease both Customs and Excise to tacksmen, while in England they were gathered in by government officials. In the circumstances it had been decided that the English method should be followed in both countries, but this raised a difficulty. In Scotland the English method was not understood, and it was therefore necessary to provide officials from England. To improvise a band of qualified officials, however, was not an easy matter, and, in point of fact, those actually sent down were by all accounts a sorry set. They were 'the very scum and canalia' of their nation, says Lockhart, and he tells a story to the effect that England was suddenly relieved of its highwaymen, as they had all gone to Scotland to find places.[1] The arrangement was that, during the first three months that succeeded the 1st of May, the new method of collecting the dues should be applied only in the case of Edinburgh and its precincts. Throughout these three months the quartering of the stranger officials in the different parts of the country went on, but under difficulties. Their coming was universally regarded with dismay and indignation. 'Not only are our merchants much alarmed', wrote the Earl of Glasgow to Mar, 'but our people are in an unaccountable ferment.'[2] In Glasgow and elsewhere troops had to be sent for the protection of the objectionable officials, whose lives were in daily peril in the different districts where they were settled. So dangerous was their position, indeed, that before the three months expired the government was alarmed lest volunteers for the service should not be forth-

[1] Lockhart, *Memoirs*, pp. 223–4.
[2] *Papers of the Earl of Mar and Kellie*, p. 394.

coming.[1]   In Edinburgh there were nightly mobs that
set law at defiance.   Meanwhile, along the whole sea-
board smuggling was proceeding on a scale that meant
ruin for the revenue.   Between the 1st of May and
the beginning of July, into Glasgow alone nearly 800
tons of brandy were successfully smuggled.   It was
the beginning of an illicit trade which was condoned
if not approved by the majority of the nation.   Smuggling became in fact a national business, and to inform
against a smuggler was to risk both person and repute.
The sympathies of the people in the incident of the
Porteous Mob as late as 1736 are a striking commentary on the light in which smuggling was generally
regarded in the country.   But the fact to be borne in
mind in connexion with the immigration of the English
officials is that, as much as any other cause, it created
a fixed antipathy to the Union in Scotland at large.
To the present day, the designations 'tide-waiter' and
'exciseman' are bywords of contempt in Scotland.

Another untoward circumstance that further pre-
judiced the Scots against the Union had its ludicrous
as well as its serious side.   As we saw, by an article
in the Treaty of Union a sum known as the Equivalent
was assigned to Scotland as a compensation for her
past losses and her future obligations.   As finally arranged, more than half of the total sum (£398,085 10s.)
was to be allocated to the African Company to recoup
their losses entailed by the failure of the Darien
scheme; part was to go for losses in connexion with
the change of the coinage, part to the payment of
national debts, and part to the expenses of the two
Commissions for Union, while £2,000 was to be

[1] *Papers of the Earl of Mar and Kellie*, p. 412.

granted annually during seven years for the encouragement of the manufacture of wool.   By the opponents
of the Union the Equivalent was denounced as a base
bribe for the sacrifice of the national independence.
Nevertheless, the Union accomplished, it was eagerly
looked for even by many who had been loudest in their
reprobation.   Knowing the state of public opinion in
Scotland, the Lord Treasurer Godolphin should have
seen to it that the money was promptly paid.   But,
as in the case of the Customs and Excise, it appeared
that no provision had been made for expediting the
business.   No date was fixed for payment, and no
commissioners were appointed for its conveyance and
distribution.   The 1st of May came, weeks passed, and
no Equivalent appeared.   'The Equivalent is so much
despaired of here', wrote one from Edinburgh, 'that
among the vulgar the greatest part believe it is gone
to Spain, and some believe that the bridge of Berwick
is fallen with the weight of it, and all is lost'[1]   At
length, on August 5, three months after the Union
came in force, conveyed in twelve waggons, and
guarded by 120 Scottish dragoons, the precious burden
reached Edinburgh, where, in spite of doubled guards,
a riotous mob vented its spleen by stoning the convoy.
Bitter was the outcry, however, when it was known
that only about a fourth of the allocated sum had been
paid in bullion—the remainder being in Exchequer
bills.[2]   Deposited for safety in the Castle, the Equivalent, though it was a welcome boon in the interests of
the country, long remained a cause of heart-burning
contention.   The four Scots who were appointed to

[1] *Papers of the Earl of Mar and Kellie*, p. 397.
[2] The bills were shortly afterwards cashed in London.

distribute it did not see eye to eye, and the distribution was tediously delayed. For the Ministers in London, also, it was a permanent source of anxiety, as it was their dread that some day it might be secured by the Jacobites, who would turn it to excellent account. Thus by ill management or, as it was expressed at the time, by 'unforeseen accidents', what was intended as a propitiation to an incensed people served only to intensify the general irritation.

Simultaneously with the trouble that arose in connexion with the Customs and the Equivalent, there was another cause of friction which, in De Foe's words, 'opened afresh the mouths' of the enemies of the Union. The result of the whole affair was that it gave occasion to a mutual suspicion between English and Scottish traders which could only be allayed after a long lapse of time. In this case, also, the misunderstanding was due to a lack of foresight on the part of the statesmen of both countries. A brief account of what took place will show how easily the mischief might have been averted. On the conclusion of the Treaty of Union an ingenious idea occurred to numerous traders both in England and Scotland. Nearly four months had to elapse before the Treaty came into force, and in the interval a profitable stroke of business might be done. The duties on imported goods were lower in Scotland than in England. Taking common counsel, therefore, these English and Scottish traders purchased large quantities of goods, especially wine and brandy, on the Continent, and landed them in Scotland, where the tacksmen, in view of the unusual quantities that passed through their hands, abated the usual dues. The meaning of this proceeding was that, as on the 1st of May the two countries would be commercially one, the imported commodities could be landed in England without the payment of further impost. But the more honest dealers in England got wind of the march being stolen upon them, and made an indignant appeal to the House of Commons, which was still only an English representative body. The House responded to the appeal and passed a bill which denounced the proceeding as 'a notorious fraud', and ruinous to her Majesty's revenue. More circumspect, however, the House of Lords rejected the bill on the ground that the English Parliament was not compe-tent to interpret the Articles of Union to which the Scottish Parliament had been a party.[1] Meanwhile the news of the Commons' action had reached Scotland, and thrown the whole trading community into a ferment. The Convention of Royal Burghs, the body charged with the commercial interests of the country, was peti-tioned to address a protest to the queen, and the Ministers of State, specially Seafield and Mar, were bitterly denounced for neglecting their country's good. Undeterred, however, by the action of the House of Commons, the Scottish traders, after securing the necessary certificates from the Commissioners of Customs in Scotland, dispatched forty ships, laden with wine and brandy, to London. On the ships appearing in the Thames they were promptly seized

---

[1] This decision of the House of Lords illustrates the point of Professor Dicey's observation : ' Though the fact is often overlooked, the Parliaments both of England and Scotland did, at the time of the Union, each transfer sovereign power to a new sovereign body, namely, the Parliament of Great Britain.'— *The Law of the Constitu-tion*, pp. 66–7, note (ed. 1908).

by the officials of the Customs. Thus it seemed that the hopes of gain from their ingenious scheme were foreclosed to the enterprising Scots. Hotly supported by the mass of their countrymen, however, they brought their complaint before the Secretary Mar, who submitted it to the queen and Council. The Treasurer Godolphin found himself in a strait place, as whatever decision the Council took, one or the other country must be exasperated. As a temporary arrangement, he suggested one of two alternatives : the Scots traders should either give bail for the arrested goods, or allow them to be deposited in cellars, of which both they and the Customs officials should have the keys. To neither of the alternatives would the Scots agree, and their pertinacity was eventually rewarded. When the first British Parliament met in the autumn, it decreed that the embargo should be taken off the arrested goods. But the mischief had been done, for it was borne in upon the traders in Scotland that they could not look for fair play from their rivals in England, who could bring so much greater influence to bear on the British Parliament.

These successive misunderstandings were not alleviated by a series of acts ostensibly in the commercial interests of both countries. As economic principles were then understood, it was inevitable that these interests should occasionally conflict. The most lucrative industries were not the same in both countries; the legislators, therefore, had to face two difficulties. An act that might favour an industry in England might not favour it in Scotland, and a tax on a certain commodity might be just in the one country and unjust in the other. 'Commercial jealousy', says Sir John Seeley,

' was in that age the dominant feeling of the English mind,'[1] and to this jealousy he ascribes the failure of England to effect a satisfactory settlement with Ireland. To Scotland, indeed, she had granted equality both in home and foreign trade, but it was natural that this dominant feeling should display itself in her relations with her new partner. Be it said that the Scottish representatives, both in the House of Commons and the House of Lords, did little to serve the interests of their country. The same divisions among them existed after as before the Union. The Court Party continued as subservient as ever to the government of the day; the Squadrone made it their persistent endeavour to thwart them; and the Jacobites lost no opportunity of fomenting misunderstandings and discrediting the Union. In view of the discordant opinions of her representatives, English Ministers might well be puzzled to know what was the true mind of Scotland on any national question that might arise.

In 1711 was passed a series of measures affecting Scottish trade which the nation regarded as contrary to its interests and even involving a breach of both the letter and the spirit of the Treaty of Union. In the case of an act relative to the manufacture of linen we have an illustration how the commercial interests of the two countries appeared to conflict. By this act a duty was imposed on the export of linen for a period of thirty-two years. But linen was for Scotland what wool was for England—its staple commodity of export; and the tax, therefore, would fall more heavily on the poorer country. When the Scottish members naturally protested against the measure, an English member

[1] *The Growth of British Policy*, ii, pp. 339, 367.

expressed what was the general feeling of his countrymen.   Scotland, he said, was now subject to England,
and must be governed by English laws.[1]   In connexion
with the same manufacture, the Scots made a loud
complaint against another bill.   For a space of five
years linen exported from Ireland to the American
Colonies had been free of duty, and the bill proposed
that the exemption should be continued for six years
longer.   Against this proposal, so disadvantageous
to their country some Scottish members vehemently
protested, and the bill was accordingly dropped for
a time, though at a later date it was passed into law.
Quite in keeping with the economical notions of the
age was the rejection of another bill specially intended
to develop a branch of Scottish industry.   In the
Highlands of Scotland there was abundance of natural
timber, and it was the object of the bill to make it
legal to import it into England for building ships for
the navy.   The importation of Scottish timber, however, would have injured the English traders who
imported timber from America, and the House of
Commons would not have the bill.   Even more bitter
feeling was roused in Scotland by what was considered
a grievous neglect on the part of the central government.   Prohibition of victual of all kinds from Ireland
had been a standing policy of Scotland for over half
a century,[2] and Parliament and Privy Council had
done their utmost to enforce the law.   Since the Union,
however, Irish victual had been surreptitiously imported in such quantities that an address, signed by
the most influential men in the country, was sent to

---

[1] Lockhart, *Memoirs*, i. 330.
[2] The same prohibition existed in England.

the queen to represent the culpable neglect of the authorities.[1]

But it was a measure passed in 1713, the year before the close of the reign, that convinced the Scottish people that the Union was an unequal yoke. The national drink of the country was ale, and, previous to the Union, it had been the anxious consideration of the legislature that it should be sold at a low price. So long as the people could have their ale cheap, the government knew there was little danger of general discontent. By the act in question, known as the Malt Tax, an equal duty was to be raised on malt in all three countries. But the barley raised in Scotland was greatly inferior to that of England; and to impose an equal tax on malt in the case of both countries was a manifest injustice. For once the Scottish members of both Houses united in opposing the measure, and the English Ministers were warned by Scotsmen of all shades of opinion that its passing might have serious consequences. Passed the measure was, however, with the support of English Whigs and Tories alike, and the immediate result, as we shall see, was an attempt to undo the Union.

Dissatisfied with what had been done for them in the way of legislation, Scottish traders had still other grounds of complaint. Among the benefits expected from the Union was the protection of trading vessels from the privateers who then swarmed in the adjoining seas. From the earliest times the foreign trade of the country had been grievously crippled through the want of a sufficient naval force to protect vessels from the attacks of pirates. The arrangement in the past had

[1] *Portland MSS.* (Hist. MSS. Com.), v, pp. 81, 96.

been that the foreign staple port with which most business was done should twice in the year send two armed ships as a convoy for trading-vessels leaving Scottish ports. The staple port at this time was Campvere in Holland, but the authorities there had failed to send the necessary convoys, with the result that many Scottish vessels fell into the hands of privateers. And not only in crossing the German Ocean, but even in sailing from one harbour to another on the Scottish coast, so many craft were seized that a voyage was a veritable running of the gauntlet. And what aggravated the grievance was that the cause of the mischief was England's war with France, in which Scotland had little interest, for it was French privateers who were on the watch for prey. It was with well-grounded reason, therefore, that the Convention of Royal Burghs addressed letters to Prince George of Denmark and Godolphin, complaining of the neglect of the government and petitioning that the Scottish coasts should have their share of protection as well as the coasts of England.[1]

In another way Scotland had suffered from England's prolonged war with France. Before the Union of the Crowns, on the occasion of the marriage of Queen Mary to Francis II, Frenchmen and Scots had become naturalized citizens of their respective countries, and, as a consequence, Scotsmen resident in France were free of the *droit d'aubaine*, and Scottish vessels paid no dues in French ports. These privileges Scotland enjoyed till 1663, when the relations of England to France occasioned their withdrawal. She still retained certain trading privileges with France, however, but

[1] *Records of the Convention of Royal Burghs*, iii, pp. 45, 46, 47.

on the outbreak of the war of the Grand Alliance in 1702 these privileges were also withheld. France had always been one of Scotland's best customers for fish and wool, two of her most lucrative commodities. It was only the Royal Burghs that had the privilege of foreign trade in the case of more valuable wares, and the embargo on these wares on the part of France was a serious drawback to their prosperity. In 1710, when the Tory government of Harley and Bolingbroke was making overtures of peace to the French, the Convention of the Royal Burghs took occasion to represent to the queen the pressing need of more favourable commercial relations with France for her northern kingdom. Again, when in 1712 the Duke of Hamilton was appointed to negotiate the preliminaries to the Treaty of Utrecht, the Convention addressed to him an urgent appeal to the same purport [1], but the Treaty of Utrecht was not concluded till the spring of 1713, the year before Anne's death. Thus throughout her reign Scotland paid the penalty of a war which the majority of her people regarded with indifference and even with disapproval.

II

The dissatisfaction of the trading community in Scotland was occasioned partly by the neglect of the government and partly by the application of mistaken economical principles. In the case of the Church, on the other hand, there appeared to be a deliberate policy to destroy its constitution and to break up its

[1] *Records of the Convention of Royal Burghs*, iii, p. 499; iv, p. 83.

communion. To set up Episcopacy in place of Presbytery seemed, even in the eyes of the saner leaders of the existing establishment, to be the ultimate aim of Anne and her English advisers. The suspicion could not but be strengthened by their knowledge of Anne's passionate attachment to the English Church, and of the fact that her immediate ancestors had detested Presbytery as incompatible with the royal prerogative. It was a risky policy to pursue if the Union was to remain intact. But for the wiser heads in the Scottish Church, and notably but for Carstares, the probability is that the Union would not have taken place. The great majority of the ministers had been against it, and, with the power they exercised over their congregations, they might have forced on a general rising which would have resulted in civil war. If the Union was to be maintained, therefore, it would seem to have been the policy of the government to conciliate the Church by all the means in its power.

The Union had not existed for a year, however, before the Church had reason to be disquieted for its future security. It was the abolition of the Scottish Privy Council in 1708 that first raised a feeling of uneasiness, for, as Carstares saw, they were now without an intermediate body between them and the government in London.[1] A ruder shock came in the following year, 1709. An Episcopalian clergyman, named Greenshields, openly read the English Liturgy in a congregation of his own communion in Edinburgh. The very name *Liturgy* was of sinister suggestion to

[1] *Carstares State Papers*, pp. 770–1; *Seafield Correspondence* (Scot. Hist. Soc.), pp. 436–7.

the great majority of the Scottish people. It was the attempt of Charles I to introduce a liturgy that had roused the nation against him, and during the ascendancy of Episcopacy in the reigns of Charles II and James VII it was considered imprudent to repeat the experiment. Only two years before, the General Assembly had passed an act specially intended to prevent the use of a liturgy in churches, either Presbyterian or Episcopal, and in so doing reckoned on the support of the state.[1] Prohibited in succession by the Presbytery of Edinburgh, by the Town Council, and by the Court of Session, Greenshields took a step that struck the Church with dismay. He appealed to the House of Lords, and that judicial body gave decision in his favour. To the Church it now appeared that the Act of Security which had been attached to the Treaty of Union as an inviolable safeguard of its constitution was a futile guarantee, and it soon had further reason for its apprehension.

In 1712 were passed two acts which convinced the Church as a body that the results of the Union were to justify all their fears. The one was an Act of Toleration that granted complete freedom of worship to Episcopalians in Scotland. Abstractly considered, the act was admirable, but less admirable were the motives that prompted it. Toleration, as we know, was equally obnoxious to the main body of Presbyterians and Episcopalians, both in England and Scotland, and was approved only by the Church that happened to need it.[2] It was from no enlightened

---

[1] The majority of the Scottish Episcopalians themselves disapproved of Greenshields's proceeding.

[2] A preacher before the General Assembly which met in May,

views of liberty of thought that the Tory government of the day decreed that toleration was to prevail in Scotland. It was the same government that had passed the Occasional Conformity Act, which deprived English Dissenters of the rights of citizenship, and the Schism Act, which disabled them from maintaining schools for the education of their own children. If we are to credit the Jacobite Lockhart, it was he who prevailed on the Ministry to give its support to the bill, and he frankly states his object in promoting it : it was, in his own words, to convince the Presbyterian clergy ' that the establishment of their Kirk would in time be overturned, as it was obvious that the security thereof was not so thoroughly established by the Union as they imagined.' [1]   Another clause in the same act at once struck at a fundamental principle of the Scottish Church, and acted as a dividing sword between her adherents. By this clause Presbyterian and Episcopalian alike were commanded to pray for the queen, and to take the oath of allegiance and abjuration—the latter, as defined by the Act of Settlement, implying that the sovereign should be an Episcopalian. Thus, in the opinion of her clergy, was the Church's spiritual independence assailed from another side, since a compulsory oath was a constraining of conscience against which she had done battle since she had come into existence. As time was to prove, the Abjuration Oath, by dividing her adherents into those who were

1712, declared that ' liberty of conscience was not nor could be a blessing to any people or person.'—Wodrow, *Correspondence* (Wodrow Society), i. 281.

[1] Lockhart, *Memoirs*, i. 418.

willing and those who were unwilling to take it, was seriously to imperil her unity.[1]

The Toleration Act was immediately followed by another act which was to have a portentous history. In 1690 lay patronage had been abolished in accordance with the will of the Church as it had been established at the Revolution. In its dislike to lay patronage the Church was still of one mind, but, to the grave alarm of her most moderate leaders, an act restoring lay patronage was placed on the statute-book. Again, as men like Carstares knew, it was no desire for the welfare of the Church that prompted the legislators.[2] Their aim was purely political. Chosen by lay patrons, ministers would lose much of their influence among their parishioners, as no longer being in a position of complete independence. But the express object of those who passed the act was the same as in the case of the Act of Toleration: it would further prejudice the Church against the Union as affording no security for its conservation. No one at the time dreamt what momentous issues the Patronage Act was to entail in the future history of the Scottish nation—issues among which it is only necessary to recall the disruption of the National Church in 1843, and the startling decision of the House of Lords in 1900.

Even more disquieting to Presbyterians than the

---

[1] See App. V.

[2] Wodrow was well aware of the fact. 'But it's plain enough', he writes, 'that both it [the Patronage Bill] and the Toleration Bill come from the October Club [composed of Tories] with a design to thwart the Church of Scotland, and to stir up confusions and disgusts at the Government, and pave the way for the Pretender.'— *Analecta*, iii, p. 33.

Toleration and Patronage Acts was an unaccountable proceeding of the Privy Council. For many years the privilege of printing the Bible had been held by a family of the name of Anderson resident in Edinburgh. For reasons which are not recorded, the Council deprived the Andersons of their privilege, and granted it to persons who are described as ' one Papist, one non-juror, and a whole society of men declared enemies to the Church of Scotland and the Revolution'. Naturally this action was generally regarded as an unmistakable indication that the ruin of the existing Church was immediately intended, and so menacing became the attitude of the ministers that De Foe, then residing in Edinburgh, thought it right to warn Oxford regarding the dangerous policy he was following.[1]

Thus, as the reign of Anne drew to its close, the Church, the most influential body in the nation, was as keenly dissatisfied with the results of the Union as the trading community. The Abjuration Oath, imposed by the British Parliament, had split it into two sections, Jurors and Non-jurors, apparently irreconcilable, and all the omens seemed to forebode that as a national institution it was doomed.[2]

III

Among other results of the Union it was anticipated that the chances of foreign invasion and rebellion

---

[1] *Portland MSS.* (Hist. MSS. Com.), vol. 5, pp. 57–8, 87–8.

[2] Writing to the Earl of Oxford on April 11, 1713, De Foe says— ' The *non-jurant* behave with rage and want of charity to the *jurant*, and are backed by the people, who, especially in the West, treat the last with insolent contempt and scarcely keep the peace with them ...' *Ib.*, p. 277.

would be at least diminished. This anticipation, as we have seen, was a leading motive in inducing England to press for the Treaty. Within a year after the Treaty had been concluded befell what had been dreaded in both countries since the beginning of the reign. In the spring of 1708 a fleet, dispatched by the French King and with the Pretender on board, appeared off the Scottish coast. A Scotsman, resident in London at the time, describes the panic occasioned by the news of the attempt, and also gives an explanation of its grounds : 'the consternation', he says, 'was very great, and the reason of it was, the great men were jealous of one another, for nobody imagined that the Pretender would venture over merely for the encouragement he had in Scotland.' The invasion was effectually frustrated, but, in view of all the circumstances that attended it, we must endorse the words of Burnet, that the issue was 'one of those happy providences for which we have much to answer'. But for a timely succession of storms the invader would have effected a landing in the Firth of Forth before the English fleet under Admiral Byng could have come up with him. By all accounts, Edinburgh would have offered little resistance, as the state of opinion in the town was such that no one was sure of his neighbour. In the whole of Scotland there were only 1,500 troops, ill-paid, ill-equipped, and probably disaffected. The enemy would have been joined by many of the Highlanders, and the episode of 1745 would have been anticipated ; if, indeed, the result might not have been more serious, seeing that the Jacobites in both countries were at once more numerous and more disposed to take risks than at the later day.

The invasion of 1708 had shown that the Union had not made Scotland less dangerous to the existing *régime*, and the years that followed were to emphasize the fact. To whatever class or section of the nation we look, the impression we receive is the same—that there was a deepening conviction that the Union had been a national misfortune, and that some other more satisfactory arrangement between the two countries must be found. In the summer of 1713 the attempt was actually made to put an end to a relation which to English and Scottish statesmen alike appeared to have become intolerable. The Malt Tax imposed in that year had convinced the commons of Scotland that under the Union prosperity was impossible, but it was from another class that the proposal to abolish it was to come.

It is an interesting fact that, in the passing of the Treaty of Union, the nobility as an order were more at one than any other class in the community. While the representatives of the shires and burghs had been nearly equally divided, a clear majority of the nobles steadily voted for the Treaty. But there was one article in the Treaty to which, as an order, they could not but object: only sixteen of them were permitted to sit in the House of Lords—an arrangement which placed them in an inferior position to the peers of England. The experience of the sixteen in the Lords' assembly was not such as to reconcile them to their position. In 1709 the Duke of Queensberry, on his being created Duke of Dover, was allowed to take his seat in the House as a peer of Great Britain. The concession in the case of Queensberry had been due to the fact that he was a subservient instrument of the

Whig government of the day. It was otherwise when, in 1711, the Duke of Hamilton claimed the same privilege on being made Duke of Brandon. English Whig and Tory peers combined to oppose the claim, and on grounds which we can understand : a Scottish peer thus privileged would have had a double vote ; he would have had his vote in the House of Lords and his vote in the election of the sixteen. Moreover, any government, if it chose, might, by making Scottish peers peers of Great Britain, have the House of Lords at its will.[1] The recently-published papers of the Earl of Mar show the seriousness of the incident as bearing on the integrity of the Union. 'If that affair of the peerage go against us,' Mar wrote to the Treasurer Oxford, 'I dread the consequence it will infallibly have. The Union depends upon it, and on the Union, with submission, depends the peace of the Queen's reign '.[2] 'We are in a harder state than you imagine,' he wrote some months later to another correspondent, 'though both parties be weary of the Union, they will upon no terms that I can see quit with the Union in a legal way.' In the following year the attempt was actually made to end the Union in 'a legal way'.[3] The man who had done as much as any other to promote the Union—the Earl of Seafield, now Earl of Findlater —moved in the House of Lords for permission to introduce a bill for its dissolution. ' There is nothing

[1] In a letter to his brother, Mar wrote : ' they [the English Lords] have such an apprehension of the acquisition of strength the Crown gets by us, and as it were in opposition to both their parties, that they will ever treat us as enemies, Whig and Tory being alike afraid of the power of the Crown.'—*Mar and Kellie Papers*, p. 495.

[2] *Ib.*, 490.   [3] *Ib.*, 494.

so like a Whig as a Tory, and nothing so like a Tory
as a Whig—a cat out of a hole and a cat in a hole'[1]
is Mar's sardonic comment on the two great political
parties of the time, and the sarcasm was illustrated by
the vote on Findlater's motion. By a majority of four,
mainly composed of Tories, the Union was saved from
peril by those who had been its most bitter opponents.

The year following the attempt to dissolve the Union
saw the close of Anne's reign. Had it been prolonged
for a few years, the probability is that a grave situation
would have arisen in Scotland. As we have seen,
there was no class or party in the country which was
not convinced that the Union had been a national
disaster. The clergy of the Established Church
clamoured for its dissolution : the Cameronians held
it in abomination ; and the Jacobites were set on the
restoration of the exiled House. What aggravated
the situation was the supine fashion in which the affairs
of the country were administered : 'here', wrote the
Earl of Kinnoull to Oxford, 'we have no Government
at all ; every one does as he pleases.'[2]   In Edinburgh
the Jacobites were in such force that they intimidated
the magistrates, and openly gave out, as they had
excellent reasons for doing, that the Queen's Ministers
were on their side.[3]   The Highland clans were kept in
submission only by liberal pensions to their chiefs,

----

[1] *Ib.*, p. 495.   Elsewhere, Mar says : 'I'm not surprised to see
some of the Whigs act the part they do in it, for being disappointed
of their design in making of the Union, and so being weary of it,
they want to make us so weary that so they may get free from it.
But for these Tories who join with them in this, all I can say of them
is, O when will they be wise !'—*Ib.*, p. 496.

[2] *Portland MSS.*, v. 256.

[3] *Ib.*, p. 76.

though it was generally suspected that the pensions were given with another object—to secure their support for the Pretender in the event of Anne's death. To that event all parties looked forward with an intensity of hope and fear to which the records of the time bear speaking testimony. How by the misunderstandings of Oxford and Bolingbroke the return of the Stewart was averted is familiar matter of English history. It was the remark of a great Whig statesman of last century that the accession of the House of Hanover was 'the greatest miracle in our history',[1] and so at the time it seems to have been regarded in Scotland. 'This strange turn of affairs we are at present under', wrote the historian Wodrow a few weeks after George I had ascended the throne, 'is so immediate an appearance of Providence as I have seen nothing like it but the happy Revolution.'[2]

In the same context Wodrow expresses the fear that the country 'was not ripe for such a deliverance', and the history of Scotland during the next quarter of a century was to justify his fear. Continued unrest in Church and State, the slow advance of national prosperity, were still attributed to the unequal yoke imposed by the Union. Not till the latter half of the century did manifest proofs show that the bond had not shackled the spirit of the nation. Then began a development of the country's natural resources unexampled in her previous history; and then also, for the first time, she took an assured place in the intellectual commonwealth of Europe. 'It is an admirable result of the human spirit,' wrote Voltaire of that

[1] Lord Morley, *Life of Walpole* (Lond., 1890), p. 40.
[2] *Correspondence,* i. 563.

period of the national history, 'that at the present time it is from Scotland we receive rules of taste in all the arts—from the epic poem to gardening.' The words were written in irony, but the actual contributions made by Scotsmen during the period to which Voltaire refers went beyond what his sarcasm implies. In literature, in speculative philosophy, in the physical sciences, they gave to the world a series of works which, in their respective spheres, mark new departures in man's thoughts regarding his own destiny and regarding his relations to the actual world.

In conclusion, we may ask a pregnant question : had Scotland rejected the Union, had she, as some of her best minds thought was her wisest course, chosen a ruler of her own and set up a kingdom independent of England, how is it likely that she would have fared ? The king she must have chosen must have been either a Protestant who was not a Stewart, or a Stewart and, therefore, a Catholic. In either event, the issue would, in all probability, have been disastrous to her. The numerous body of Catholics in the country would never have been satisfied with a king who was not of the ancient royal House. There would have been Jacobite attempts more formidable than the '15 and the '45. Supported by their numerous contingent in the Lowlands, and with the Highlands at their back, the Jacobites would in all likelihood have succeeded in overthrowing the existing government and have placed a Stewart on the throne. As the inevitable consequence, the vanquished party would have appealed to England, which in its own interests would have responded to the appeal. The Stewart would in his turn have been ejected, but the intervention of England would eventually have been resented by all Scottish parties, and the old story would have been renewed of international jealousy between the two kingdoms, to the serious detriment of both.

Such, we have every reason to conjecture, would have been the course of events had a king been chosen who was not a Stewart. The issues would not have been less disastrous had a Stewart been chosen. Equally in affairs of state and religion he would have followed the traditional policy of his family. Again, as in the previous century, there would have been a Protestant-Whig revolt, and in this event, also, England would have been called in by the insurgent party to settle accounts with their adversaries.

Whether, therefore, we look at the internal condition of Scotland at the period of the Union or at the circumstances that then obtained in Europe at large, the conclusion seems forced upon us that the Union was both necessary and desirable if she was to win her due share of the world's prosperity and to keep pace with the development of other nations. And not less necessary and desirable was the Union in the interests of England. Not with the same giant strength could she have done battle for commercial supremacy, had Scotland been her enemy and the convenient instrument of enemies still more formidable.

APPENDIXES

APPENDIX I

Letters of John Murray, 2nd Marquess, afterwards Duke of Atholl, to Godolphin.

Brit. Mus. Add. MSS. 28055.

fol. 25.]

My Lord,

. . . .

Tusday night last the Comisioner desiered the officers of staite, President of yᵉ Councill and Lords of Treasury, Lᵈ Stairs, & President of the session to come to him to considder what was to be done yᵉ next day in Parlᵐᵗ. His Grace[1] told first his owne opinion that the next day he designed to move the giving a supply for maintanance of the forces, that he believed if it were longer delayed there would more difficultys arise, that he had assurances it would then carry; in short, all then present were of yᵉ same opinion except myselfe who gave these reasons : that a competent supply would be granted in which the majority of all the parties would concur, &, therefore, the right timing of it was the principall thing ; that I thought it was the same thing to yᵉ Queen to have the supply that day or five or six days after; that, if it was first

[1] Duke of Queensberry.

pressed, it woud give a jealousie that no good Laws were designed, but that yᵉ Parˡᵗ woud be adjourned soone after, & that I thought it was better for the Queen that her servants shoud first offer and bring in any good Laws she had impowred her Comisioner to grant; that this woud be so satisfactory to the Parˡᵗ· that they woud concur unanimously in the supply when ever it was proposed, or apoint a certaine day for it. But being singly of this opinion I left yᵉ management of the debaite next day to the advisors, which was wednesday, but just before the Comissioner went to the House, the Pre: of Councill & D: Argile came to him and told him they found severals, particularly the Burrows, would have in an act ratifying the Convention of Estates, yᵉ forfieture of K. Ja:, that Convention being turned to a Parˡᵗ ratifying Presb: Goverment & aproving the legality of the last Parˡᵗ and that they both were ready to goe into this act. This was the first turn & begining of all the difficulties we are brought into & was the more surprising that the Pre: of Councill was so forward the night before to push yᵉ Comisioner to begin with the supply. The caryers on of this are the same that carryed on the abjuration, & the designe is also the same, to witt, to scar or exclude as many as possible by representing those that goe not into that act as not fitt to be assumed into yᵉ Queens service, &, if that faill, I am told there are other acts yet more strict & yᵉ abjuration also to be brought in to divide the Parˡᵗ & the nation. The House having mett wednesday yᵉ 26, the Comisioner proposed in a short speach to begin with yᵉ supply, wᶜʰ soone apeared woud not doe. The first thing opposed to it was to proceed to end the Elections, & at last Mʳ Fletcher of Salton offered a resolve to the House, viz: that before all other business whatsomever they shoud pass all acts for security of Religion, Liberty, and traide, wᶜʰ was understood both as to the Limitations of the succesour & during the Queens reigne. This was oposed all that coud be, &, after spending 7 or 8 howers in debaite or raither wrangling, the Comisioner & the rest of yᵉ Queens servants yealded to proceed upon any particoular acts for Religion, Liberty, &

traide, but then, the opposet partys finding their strength, nothing woud satisfie but the resolve. At length, about nine at night, yᵉ Comisioner adjurned yᵉ Parlᵗ without coming to any resolution or vote that day. On fryday the 28, before the Parlᵗ mett, the Comisioner and officers of state desiered yᵗ I might give in an act for the meeting of the Estaits after yᵉ Queens death. This was thought very fitt, both because there were other draughts of that nature ready to be given in with clauses wᶜʰ might be hard for the Queen to pass, such as declairing a successour yᵗ shoud not be King of England & also because it seemed absolutely nessessary to have an act more cleare then yᵉ act of the Parlᵗ (96), wᶜʰ yʳ Lᵈᵖ knows did occasion so much debaite. I send yʳ Lᵈᵖ inclosed the first draught. It was hastily done & coud not be gott ready till just yᵉ Parlᵗ was meeting. It's like there may be alterations or additions made to it in the house. The Comissioner says he thinks it reasonable it shoud pass and woud endevour to get an instruction for it. After I proposed this act we insisted that we might proceed on that and other particular Laws without being tyed up by the resolve. I said that, this being both my own opinion & now agreed to by all yᵉ Queens servants, and in the very terms of yᵉ resolve proposed, I hoped they woud be satisfied to accept of this & other good Laws without binding up the Queen & Parlᵗ by a resolve wᶜʰ woud be time anough to enter into whenever any of us proposed the supply. But the ferment and jealousie was grown to such a height that what woud have been very acceptable at first coud not then be heard, & it was plainly said, both that day & at yᵉ first days debait, that yᵉ Comissioner had in a former Parlᵗ made promieses to continue the Parlᵗ after the supply was granted, but yᵗ he did cutt them short, &, tho the Comissioner did answer this, yet it gave no satisfaction.

And now, since I have as nearly & truly as I can naratted the matter of fact, the Queen may be pleased to judge if it may not be fitt this session be as short as can be, wᶜʰ I wish may be happyly ended, which I shall contrebutte to all I can. I shall be glad to hear particularly from yʳ Lᵈᵖ what the

Queen thinks proper for her service at this juncture, wch shall be obeyed by

Y^r L^dps most faithfull
and most humble servant
ATHOLL.

Holyrood house
    May 30/1703.

[Postscript]

MY LORD

I had almost forgott to tell y^r G^r that, in the wedensdayes debaitt, one of the members, speaking of the unfittnes to be governed by an English Councill, did name the Ld Treasurer. I must doe the Justice to the Comissioner, Chancelor, D. Hamilton, as wel as my self, to acquaint y^r G^r that we all took the gentleman up very sharp. I said that, having the honour to know your G^r particularly, I was sure he coud not have instanced one in all England that was more friendly to our nation, or had juster sentiments of the united interest of both Kingdoms, so that, instead of a reflexion, there was an oppurtunity given to let all the Parl^t heare a just character of y^r G^r. . . . .

. . . .

fol. 29.]

Holyrood house
June 10/1703

MY LORD

My last to y^r G^r of the 30th went by a flying packett .

. . . .

I have & shall doe all I can to wave the limitations for the successor since they may be better done by the meeting of the Estaites when they declaire one.

Since my last to y^r G^r we have gone every day to greater & greater heates. Thursday last, when an act for tolleration was moved, the E. of Leven & E. of Marchmont, late Chancelor, did insist with a great deale of heate & indiscretion that the Queens letter to the Council concerning those of the Episcopal perswasion shoud be produced, which the Queens servants opposed as being absolutly unnecessary, & that it was known it was in the terms of Law. The Justice Clerk happning to say that calling for the letter in that manner was attacquing the Queen, those Lords & some others insisted that he shoud go to the bar, but thought fitt to let theire motion fall. At last it was yeilded the letter shoud be brought to the house, but, when it was reade, there was none coud say any thing to it.

On Monday last the act which I gave y^r G^r an accompt of before, wch was brought in by D. of Argile, was againe reade, the copie of wch is inclosed. The first part of the act concerning the meeting of the Estaites having been turned into a Parl^t I agreed to, as did all others who spoke to it, but the 2^d part as it was worded I thought woud prove of so dangerous consequence not only to those that served the Queen & the Government but also to all the other subjects, that nether the one or the other coud live in security, & therefore I, with several others, proposed that the last clause might be worded as the first is; viz. that it shoud be high treason to quarrel or impugne the dignity or Authority of the claime of Right, but not to have it high treason to speak or writte against any of the articles of itt, which might prove so ensnaring that ether an illdesigning ministry or a party in a Parl^t might forfeitte any subject in the Kingdom of life & fortune. I said that, for my part, I had observed the claime of Right exactly, both when in the government & out of itt, & that I knew none coud attacque me on that or any other accompt, & at least I shoud be as cairful for the future, but I thought nothing coud be of wors consequence then to make an act which woud put all her Maties subjects in constant feares, &, my Lord, the inconveniences are so many & so obvious that I need not repeate what I or any other said on this subject. Y^r G^r will easily make a judgement by comparing the claime of right with the act inclosed. In short, my Lord, if the act pass, the Q. & her servants may be said to committ treason against the claime of

Right or treason against the people, which is now the new language, & if the people goe to arms on pretence of the claime of Right, to oppose them will be called treason, so that the difficulties [that] may ensue are not to be exprest.

The duty & affection I have for the Queen, & the manner of her bringing me into her service has made me writte so freely on this subject, that her Matie may take what method she thinks fitt to prevent the dangers [that] may follow if the act shoud pass, & therefore I know your G^r will lay this before her Matie, that her pleasure may be signified here as soon as possible. We are longing much for a good conclusion soon to this session of Par^lt, especially since the season makes it more agreable to be in the Country.

If it has been used as an argument for the act that it was voted by a great plurality, that cannot be properly said, because the first vote concerning it was 'proceed' or 'delay' to the next meeting. It carried 'proceed' but by 21 votes, after wch many members left the house, thinking, when so reasonable a desire as one days delay was not granted, it was not necessar to insist further, & I must observe that it was carried on so fast that the claime of Right was not so much as reade in the house. I am, my Lord, Y^r G^rs

most faithfull & most humble servant

ATHOLL.

fol. 33.]

MY LORD,

Since y^r G^r sayes the Queen does not incline to part with the prerogatives of the crown, tho they shoud not take place till after her decease, I shall not insist on them, & doe what I can that others may not, for I find her Maties inclinations does determine me fully, especially since I find by y^r G^r she continues her good opinion of me.

I hope the Queens servants will hereafter concur in what relaites to her Matie. If I shal happen to differ, the Queen is

Judge, & I am sure it shal be on a full perswassion that its most for her service. As I differed concerning the last part of the act given in by D. of Argile as I writt in my last particularly my own sentiments, which perhaps I relaite too fully, but it is to prevent any mistake may afterwards be alledged as to my cariadge wch my letters will cleare. The Queens other servants that concurred in my opinion as to that act were the Chancelor, V. Tarbat, & Lord Justice Clerke. The last & I voted against the clause. V. Tarbat, I think, was *non liquet*. The Chancelor as being president, y^r G^r knows, does not vote, but spoke indeed very well & very fully against it. Yesterday we had nothing before us but Elections. L^{tt} General Ramsayes was one which is not yett ended. It consists of several points, some of which are well founded, others not, & therefore I voted against him in one. Monday next is apointed for private bussines.

I am,

My Lord, &c.

ATHOLL.

Holyrood hous, June 12/1703.

I forgott to acquaint y^r G^r that I gave in an act last week against imposing New Oaths, wch I find are still designed by a party to keep themselves in & exclude as many as they can. Since I had the use of my reason, I have alwayes [been] against them. They debauch consciences, brings judgements on a nation, & are of no real advantage to a government.

fol. 37.]

Holyrood house,

June 19, 1703.

MY LORD,

I writt to your G^r last post that my patent was sent up, which indeed I gave the Commissioner at his own desire, who promised to send it by the last post, but since his G^r has failed to me once, I doe not know but he may againe, & therefore I have sent another copie to Mr Nairne, being confident that the Queen, who was so good & just to her promise as to signe it before, will doe it againe & send her orders that it may pass before any others as I writt to y^r G^r in my last, for now the Comissioner owns he has another patent for a Duke to the Mar. of Douglas wch he designes shoud be first passed, because he is come of his family, wch indeed was a very good reason why D. Queensberry ought not to have been made a Duke before the heads of his family. But I hope the Queen will not think it reasonable to prefer D: Queens: freind & relation to her own servant & one who has the great honour to be one of her own family, especially since I cautioned the Queen when I askt this honour that it was like others might pretend to the same title, & that was the only reason if she thought fitt that I desiered it might be done when I spoke to her Matie whoes answer was that I having spoke first, mine shoud be passed first, but belived it might be more convenient for her service to delay it until the Par^{lt} was over, which I immediatly & readily acquiesced to, and said that I knew that was as sure as if it were then done, so, as I did then, I doe still depend wholy on the Queen, expecting her Maties orders for passing my patent first & humbly begs pardon for this trouble wch y^r G^r sees I am forced to. This day we have been againe on the elections. The $Parl^t$ is adjourned to tuesday & then I hope we shal goe to publick bussines, wch is more then time considdering we have satt 7 weeks. I am afraide our factions will not decrease, but on the conterar. I intend to writte particularly to y^r G^r soon by a sure occasion, who am, My Lord,

&c.

ATHOLL.

The Mar: of Douglas is but a child of 8 or 9 years old.

fol. 39.]

Holyrood house,
June 26, 1703.

MY LORD,

My son Tullibardine is bearer of this, who I have allowed to goe to the Camp comanded by D. Marlborough, to whom I have writt that his G^r will be pleased to concern himself in him & to renew the proposal I made a good time agoe for my son. Lady Mary Churchil being so young, I hope Duke & Dutches of Marlborough are not engadged, & I must own that the greatest motive I have in this is that theire other daughters prove so good wives, & that I know they have good example & vertuous education, besides I think my self oblidged to persue the designes of most kind parents, who had a particular respect & kindnes for D. & Dut: of Marlborough. Y^r G^r was the first that I acquainted with my inclinations in this matter & I beg leave to intreate y^r assistance as ye person I alwayes rely on in my greatest concerns. I have writt so long a letter to E. Nottingam, wch I doubt not he will comunicat to y^r G^r, that I shall not begin to enter on Parl^t affaires in this but tell y^r G^r that I cannot but be more and more of the opinion that the passing of the act relating to the claim of Right in the terms it is voted may prove extreamly inconvenient to the Queen, &, tho it be true that it may be inconvenient not to pass it after it is voted, yett I am convinced the other will be greater. The worst is that there may be Addresses to desire the Queen to pass itt. But I am sure there will be many more Addresses to thank her Matie if she does not. And as for any noise may be made in Eng: about it, it must satisfie all reasonable people that there can be no absolute necessity for this act, otherwayes why have not the party that has now caryed it desired it in all the late Reigne. And in the next session of Parl^t I doubt not but the act will be voted in the terms I formerly writt, for none disagrees to the first part, nor will to the second if it be expressed that it shal be treason to quarrel the Authority of the claime of Right. This is in answer to the last of the 19 I have the honour to receave from y^r G^r in wch you seem to think the inconveniency of not passing itt will be great, & that there may be another opportunity of remidying, but we have a Scots proverb I often find true, that its better holding then drawing.

My son will give y^r G^r an accompt of what has passed publickly in Parl^t & how the Com: has used me in relation to the patent. I heare he sent up a flying packett about it, monday last, without acquainting me, tho I have the honour to be an officer of Staite, & lodged very neare him.

I am, My Lord,

&c.

ATHOLL.

fol. 44.]

Holyrood house,
July 10.

MY LORD,

I have just heard of a flying packett to be dispatched, & therfore can only acknowledge the honour of y^r G^{rs} of June 27 in answer to the first I had writt about the patent, as to wch I shall say nothing now untill I heare againe, but that it seems y^r G^r had mistaken me as if I had pressed it might pass before the Par^{lt} shoud rise, wch I did not designe. And as to the precedency, when the Queen is minded that none was in competition when I spoke nor long after, I am ready to receave her determination, which shal alwayes be satisfactory to me.

I doubt not but the Comissioner & others have given y^r G^r an accompt of the late proceedings in Parl^t. We have all concurred, I meane the Queens servants, to keepe the limitations out of the act of security, which we have done with a great deale of difficulty, & in which I am sure I have done all I coud both by my self & friends that are of the Cavalier party without whoes assistance they had certainly been votted before this time, particularly the act lodging the power of declaring Peace & War in the Par^{lt} after her Maties decease wthout aires. As this appeares most necessar, so it is the first is pressed, but none can answer but others will be insisted on. But at least it may be reckoned that this will carry, & by yesterdayes resolve it is to come in immediatly after the rest of the elections are finished & which are to follow the act for security &, when the time for bringing in this act of Peace & War was reasoned yesterday, the Queens servants & Comissioners freinds did first yeild that it shoud be considered this session of Par^lt & particularly the Lord Stairs, because, I suppose, he saw it coud not be shunned, & afterwards the Ld Register did yeild it shoud be considered before the suply, after which there was no room for reasoning or voting, for it was thought no great difference since it was to come in before the suply whither it was just after the elections or some dayes longer, since the Queen can now be acquainted & her Maties resolutions known before it can be brought in. And this was the reason I did not votte, thinking itt unfitt to predetermine ourselves by a resolve in the middle of an act, especially [as] after it was yeilded there was no probability of retriving. This I have acquainted y^r G^r off, because I have alwayes found, since the minut that the Queen named me to her service without my aplying my self to her ministers here, it has been some of theire endeavour to misrepresent me on every occasion, as particularly I heare by alledging that my freinds goe on way & I another, tho I doe act for the Queens service. This is hard to impute other persons actions to me, for tho some of my freinds doe not concur with me, wch I am sure I cannot help, yett it is certaine, if I had not had influence on severals, things had broke out into greater extreams then they have done, & particularly the Par^lt had been in the greatest heate that ever it was known in if I had not concurred with the Chancelor to bring the Comissioner out of the difficulty he was in by refusing to accept of the Lord Belhavens & Sr Alex: Ogilvies submission, & which I heare also was misrepresented, but it was easie to judge that nothing coud irritate a Par^lt more then keeping not theire members, wch was not possible to be done without theire own consent, &, tho those two persons crimes were not justifiable, yett the punishment of giving them an indictment on high treason appeared too great for the offence. Butt at last the Comissioner thought it fitt to accept of a submission wch was done in as humble a manner as possible, but I beg pardon for having insisted on these things especially since I am convinced that I serve a mistres [who] will not misconstruct her servants without examining what they can say for them selves. I shal conclude this with repeating that the factions & humours are so great that I heartily wish this Par^lt came soon to a good conclusion, &, if the Queen do not resolve to give the assent to any limitations, it is best preventing the votes.

> I am, My Lord,
>> &c.
>>> ATHOLL.

My son writt to me he had waitted on y^r G^r and delivered my letter. I shall long to have the Dut: of Marl: & y^r G^rs answers. Y^r letters come safe under the Chancelors covers.

fol. 54.]

MY LORD,

We have been expecting an answer to the last flying packett to kno her Maties pleasure as to the passing the act of security, as to wch I writt fully to y^r G^r then, therfor shall not ad much to itt, but that you may immagine since there was so much zeale & heate in the Par^lt to gett this act, it will be a very great disapointment if it shoud not be. Itt may make the ministry here have no interrest ether to carry the suply in this Par^lt, or perhaps in any other. But, on the other hand, if the Queen does consent to it, this session, I doubt not, will conclude immediatly by giving suplies for the army. But without the act be passed or assurances that it will, we find they will not enter on the suplies, but I am afraid will enter on new acts that will be more & more uneasie. Therfore I am sure itt is the Queens interrest to put a conclusion as soon as possible ether by allowing the act to be passed or, if her Matie is perswaded it may prejudice her affaires more elswhere then advance them here, then still it is fitt her pleasure be known as soon as possible that we may be adjourned.

Since the act was voted, we have gone on pritty easily as I formerly writt was promised us, except as to the entering into the last branch of our resolve, wch is trade, which we did what we coud to enter into, both to bring the Par^lt the sooner to a conclusion, & to prevent several very unreasonable acts were proposed under the 2^d branch of the resolve, wch was liberty.   I hope the Comissioner has done me the justice to acquaint y^r G^r I have been assisting in this & without wch the Par^lt had broke up abruptly.   I heard there was a flying packet came wth a letter from y^r G^r a few dayes before the Queen went to the Bath.   The Comissioner did not acquaint me nor, I belive, the Chancelor or Ld Tarbat wth the contents of it ; wherfore, if I have writt anything that is not agreable to the Queens directions by that express, itt is for want of knowing itt.   I am,

My Lord,

&c.

ATHOLL.

Holyrood house, Sept: 1, 1703.

fol. 58.]

MY LORD,

The Par^lt was adjourned thursday last, wch I belive will be no surprise, considering how long it has satt, & what strugles & difficulties we have mett with, w^ch, since it was evident were daily increasing instead of decreasing, the Chancelor, V. Tarbat, & I, as I writt in my last, did give our opinion to the Comissioner that we thought it better to adjourn then to continue longer & involve the Queen in new difficulties by giving the negative, but the Comissioner resolved to try againe if the suplies coud be granted.   Accordingly, on wedensday they were proposed, but very unreasonable limitations, which were first given in by Mr Fletcher of Salton & afterwards proposed by the Mar: of Montrose, were againe insisted on & opposed to the suplies, but, before it was voted wch we shoud proceed to, the Mar: of Montrose past from the staite of the vote they had first given in & proposed they might proceed to liberty, wch we saw was but a more plausible & general term & woud include the limitations, &, if that had been once voted, we had been of new engadged, wherfore the Comissioner durst not venture to put that to the votte, but desiered I might propose a delay untill he shoud consider what method was next to be taken. Accordingly I proposed to delay the question till next meeting, wch was acquiesced to, & next morning the Comissioner came to my chamber, I having fallen ill that night, & told me he found it was impracticable to insist on suplies at this time & therfore resolved to adjourn the Par^lt, as accordingly he did. I shall ad no more now since I shall more fully by an express wch is to goe soon.

I am, My Lord,
&c.
ATHOLL.

Holyrood house, Sept. 18, 1703.

fol. 60.]

Holyrood house Sept: 21, 1703.

MY LORD,

My last to y^r G^r was designed to have gone by a flying packett, but I heare some of the Comissioners servants gave it to the Lord Ross who was to ride post, but I suppose will not reach London so soon as the flying packett. Its probable that, now that the Par^lt is up, there will be misrepresentations made, for, since the undertakers coud not make good what was promised, the blame must be laied off themselves on som others. But, that y^r G^r may know the true matter of fact, the Chancelor, V. Tarbat, now E. of Cromarty, & I have sent the bearer Mr Ogilby of Boine to inform y^r G^r of what has passed both in Par^lt & at our meetings. He represents one of our shires in the North, & has gone alongst wth the Queens servants in every thing relaited to her Matie the whole Par^lt & with whoes cariadge the Comissioner as well as we are fully satisfied, for, tho som of the Cavalier party, of wch this gentleman is one, did somtimes differ from us, yett this gentleman did never differ from the Court in one Votte wherin

the Queen was concerned, & was besides very assistant to us
in keeping others of that party in theire duty, & who I did
countenance & encouradge on these accompts, that they shoued
theire forwardnes in serving the Queen, first by promising not
to quarell the legality of the last Par^lt. In the next place,
they joined in Recognising the Queens title & Authority, and,
in the 3^d place, gave in the act for the suply very early in the
Par^lt. What occasioned many of them to differ with us afterwards I shal not mention, but they say that the Comissioner
did not keep his promises to them, & encouradged thoes that
brought in acts to be uneasie to them & forced them to joine
with the Country party. I shall now say that I have also done
all I coud to make both them and the Country party easie,
notwithstanding the Queen has not given the assent to the act
of security, & in this have succeeded better then coud be
imagined, for not only the members of Par^lt but others show
a great inclination to be easie in hopes the Queen will in time
ether be satisfied to pass that act as it is or, if she cannot, that
her Matie will take such measures as will make both her and
the Nation easie.

My Lord, I must beg leave to acquaint y^r G^r that I am
much surprised to heare from the Comissioner that he had
received orders to delay giving me up my patent. I cannot
but think it must be a mistake, considering what the Queen
said to me when she was pleased to grant me that honour, &
also what the Dutches of Marlborough & y^r G^r has since writt
to me about it that it was to be given me immediatly after the
Par^lt. The Comissioner has indeed showed me a postcript of
one of y^r G^r letters in wch y^r G^r writtes that the patents of
honour may be taken back when he returns to London, but
I am perswaded y^r G^r did not intend that shoud relaite to my
patent. The Comissioner tells me he expects a flying packett
every day with orders to give it up, but, if there be none, I
hope y^r G^r will see that there be justice done me in that
matter w^ch, especially now after it is publickly known, woud
be putting a particular afront on me.

I shall ad no more but tell y^r G^r that the Chancelor

acquainted me that he had writt that it was proper the Queen shoud send for me to advise what measures were to be taken in Scotts affaires. I assure y^r [Grace] I knew nothing of this untill after he had writt, & my particular circumstances in having been so litle at home, & now, after my fathers death, will make another London journy most inconvenient to me. But, if it be thought I can contribute to put her Maties affaires on a good foot, I shall rather cross both my own inclinations, & suffer the loss to my private affaires then decline to serve the Queen if she thinks it necessar.

I am My Lord
&c.
ATHOLL.

My Lord,

Since writing the inclosed I have the honour of y^r G^rs of the 17th in wch y^r G^r acquaints me that the Queen had ordered y^r G^r to tell me that her Matie was very well pleased with my service in opposing the Adress for her Assent to the act of security. It is a great satisfaction that her Matie incouradges her servants when they doe there duty, and on this occasion I shall also tell y^r G^r that I have hindered an Adres was designed after the Par^lts rising, but I shal ad no more particulars, since y^r G^r writtes in your last that the Queen expects the Chancelor & I to attend her Matie after the Par^lt rises. This with what y^r G^r writt to the Chancelor in a former letter, together with the Queens instructions to the Comissioner, has determined the Chancelor & me to waitte on the Queen as soon as we can, however uneasie it may be in my circumstances.

fol. 64.]

Belford, Oct: 3, 1703.

My Lord,

The Chancelor & I are come this far on our journy to attend the Queen, whoes affaires in Scott: we have jointly endeavored to setle & have left them more quiett then coud have been expected considering the heates & animosities were in the late Par^lt. The D: of Queensberry thought fitt at last to deliver me up the patent the Queen was pleased to grant me. I find my self so much oblidged to her Matie for her goodnes in that honour she has done me that I am impatient to assure her Matie that I have a most grateful sense of it, by wch she has engadged me and my family to be still more & more dutiful to her. This is all I shall ad since I hope, if please God, to wait on y^r G^r about the middle of the month at London & to assure y^r G^r that I shall alwayes continue,

My Lord, &c.

ATHOLL.

APPENDIX II

Letters of James Johnstone, Lord Clerk Register of Scotland, to Godolphin.

Brit. Museum Add. MSS. 28055.

fol. 84.]

[Edinburgh,] 18 June, 1704.

MY LORD,

The bearer is Mr Wedderburne. Its necessary that the adjournment be to the sixt as the Commissioner desires, for one days session of par̃t. without the burrows would looke strange, and their meeting is fixed by act of par̃t.

Its fit the two orders about Mr Wedderburne and Sr D. Nairn be dispatched that my Ld Cromarty may be gone; and the order of adjournment must be sent by a flyeing packett this night. As to the convoy, my Ld Tweddale would make a strange figure without his Equipage, and the Scotch frigate may be at Orkney, and it will look odd to refuse him a convoy for half a days saylling, that is, from Newcastle to the Basse, whereas former Com^{rs} used to have convoys & often yaughts too, even from the Thames. We can send an order to Newcastle by land for the ships of war incase they be gone. Its fit I know when your Lōp comes to town.

I am,

&c.

J. JOHNSTOUN.

fol. 90.]

Edinburgh, July ye 8, 1704.

MY LORD,

I wrong'd my eyes with posting, which oblidges me to use another hand, and, indeed, my owne is so bad that I hope your Lordshipp will very readily forgive my not useing it. I was of opinion at London, as you may remember, that

matters here were in a very bad state, but I did not think it
half so bad as I have found it. I have met with amongst the
gennerality as it were a crye against the Queens measures and
with a diffidence and dispondancy amongst those few that
were for them. The D. of Q—rys Actings in his last month
have given the country party, as we speak, a jealoussy not to
be removed but with time, and have made the honest men
amongst them dispair of reformation. Then there is, as it
were, a conspiracy of all sides to believe that the Queen is not
for the succession, which, indeed, is the received doctrin. I
may add to your Lordshipp, who loves to know the trueth,
that the prevailing growing spirit here is averst to the succession, and many of those that would be for it at another time
call the indeavouring of it now a servill complyance with the
hous of lords. But, my Lord, notwithstanding these difficulties,
I have, ever since I came, mentained to all those I have mett
with that the Queens measures would carry in parliament if
we took time anough to make them be understood, and did
not begin with the plot. For near ten days I was in a manner
alone of this opinion, but now a great many are of it, and
without doubt the business in hand is capable of a management that will make it succeed even without the two Dukes,
whom I do not at all reckon apon, but I owne that the
management is very nice, and that, if we, the Queens servants,
hit apon it, we may impute the success to those kind stars that
it seems at present superintend her Maj^{ties} affairs everywhere.
Your Lordshipp will alow me here to wish the Dutchess of
Marlborough joy. That which I apprehend most in our
business is the parliaments insisting on reparation to the
Affrican Company for their losses in Caledonia. All the
Burrows, and, I think, the majority of the other members are
concerned in this. Their losses are great, but less will sattisfie.
It seems fit that the Commissioner know something of her
Maj^{ties} mind in this matter.

I am,

&c.

J. JOHNSTOUN.

fol. 103.]

Ed^r, 19 July, 1704.

My Lord,

Had I any thing but defeats to write of, I would have presumed to write to her Ma^{ty}, and I am apprehensive that your Lo^p will rather think that I write too much to you. One thing I must ad to the Memoriall, that here Mr Secretary Harleys name has been made use of, justly or unjustly I know not, as if he had let out hopes of mighty things to be got by a Treaty which has done much hurt. I know he has prejudices to me and he dissembles them not, but sure those cannot dispose him to wrong such a national concern as this. I wished him joye upon his preferment and offered to informe him of Scotch businesse (and desired his assistance), for I know he is abused by litle people ; upon which he said he would be with me the next day, but, I adding that he must bring me a message from your Lōp without which I could not open my self to him, he nither came nor could I ever find him tho I sought him often. If he has any better scheme to setle this nation than what is proposed, I shall be glad to know it and to joine in it. I am ashamed to write to the Duchess of Marlborough, tho I need her Tokai wine mightily.

I wish your Lōp much joy of the garter and am, with all respect,

Your Lōps
&c.
J. Johnstoun.

The plot is moved for to have a fling at the house of Lords and at My ̃d Levin because he acts sincerely on the succession, but the new party will defend him in opposition to Athol.

fol. 107.]

Ed^r, 22 July, 1704.

My Lord,

I have the honour of yours & have seen yours to the Com^r & Chan^r, and it is enough that the managers are convinced (which I have always assured them of) that the Queen will steadily prosecute the measures laid down. There is noe doubt of the Event, but I humblie beg that the Queen may be prevailed with to yield to expedients for a temper [?] betwixt what, on the one hand, we deserve, and which may be fit to be done by her Ma^{ty} as She is stated in England, and what, on the other hand, is fit to be done for the good of this nation and bringing them to their witts again. Sure, if her Ma^{ty} knew of remedys sufficient to recover her subjects in Bedlam, she would not upon consideration forreigne to them omit the applying of those remidys. All will end well with tyme and wisdome & her Ma^{tys} starrs. Resentments should fall upon persons; they deserve them, but it is hard if they appear in measures that will make the innocent herd suffer, for this nation is at present fuell ready to take flame if fire must be put to it. France will doe it, but I hope it is in her Matys power, as noe doubt it is in her heart, to prevent that.

My Lord, I never thought it possible to compasse the succession or any settlement here but by the union of the new party and the Revolutioners, which union now cannot faill, but the way to come at it was not by shewing favour to the D. of Q^{ry}, for he has made use of this to perswade people here that he was to be in power again, provided they made the present measures faill. His personal interest is nothing, but this expectation, on the one hand, made many of his side opposers and, on the other hand, threw back many of the new party to the Cavaliers; besides the strenth of his friendships lay amongst men who suffered him to make use of their names, but who own that he knew they were agst the succession. Nay, its plain now that he has been all along in a formed design agst it, tho his Interest of security money will not be got and so gentle methods will not be practicable, without which, considering the present temper and disposition, all will goe to confusion or violence, whereas, if money be given and the parł end calmly and during a recess, the nation have pledges or, at least, a prospect of a good government. Morally speaking, matters must come right the next session.

There were great heats in part yesterday, my silence having been misconstrued, as if I was so guilty of I know not what that I durst not speake. I own that I took a large share in the heats that happened and I beleive I have put an end to them as to my self. But reflexions went so far betwixt one Sʳ Jˢ Halkett and Mʳ ffletcher that the part made them both give their parole of honour to carry the matter noe further. The heatts were the more violent that they were amongst friends— for the old party, except My Lᵈ Argyle, only lookt on. The Marquess of Montrosse and his friends joined with the new partye not only in Voting, for he himself spoke several tymes, which did much good. He and they are positive that, if the act of security be past, it will not be in the power of the 3 Dukes (for so we speak) to spoill matters in another session.

I am,

&c.

J. JOHNSTOUN.

fol. 114.]

26 July, 1704, Edʳ.

MY LORD,

The Queen will have full information of what past yesterday by a Memorial sent by the Comʳ. That which I have to ad is that, tho in the Theory it be verry reasonable to think that the passing of an act of security will render the nation secure and consequently lesse concerned to have a nomination, yet, when we come to particulars, this does not hold, for we know many whom the passing the act of security will gain to be for a nomination, but we cannot find those men whom the passing of that act will render either averse to it or unconcerned for it. The high Cavaliers will never be for a nomination nor indeed are concerned, whatever they pretend, whether the act of security pass or not, and therefore fell upon the invention of a treatie. Well meaning men that keep still united to them own that they are willing to leave them when- ever they are convinced by things such as the act of security or other concessions that the Court of Engl: is willing to gratifye this nation without forcing the succession upon them, which, they say, they are willing to come in to whenever they can doe it with honour, and that it comes before them without an air of compulsion.

The Revolutioners will be for the succession, whether the act of security be past or not. The new party will dwindle to nothing in case it be not past, and I doubt much if any of them in that case will accept of any employments, for, if they doe accept, they know that they will lose themselves in the opinion of the nation, for its impossible to perswade people here that the Courts reason for not passing that act is that they apprehend the passing of it will hinder the nomination, for such is the present disposition here that they will needs conclude from the not passing of that act that the Court is willing the army be disbanded and that matters run to confusion, trusting to their own strenth for remedys. This may seeme incredible at a distance, but its evident matter of fact here.

. . . .

Your Lōp will forgive me now if I write too much to you & such long and uncorrect memorialls, which often I have not tyme to read over, for we are in a strange condition here.

I am,

&c.

J. JOHNSTOUN.

fol. 118.]

27 July, 1704.

MY LORD,

In the condition we are in its hard for any man to have his thoughts about him. I have this day had occasion to be put in mind of what I forgot yesternight to write upon—the subject of the act of security. Those of the old party, at least many of them (tho not those of the best sense amongst them), are not, I now find, for the passing of that act, because they apprehend that the passing of it will beget a good understanding betwixt her Ma^{ty} and this nation, which they conclude will end in enquyryies that they are not proof for. But, not to insist that this is a false reasoning, for fresh resentments will be stronger then the humour of enquirys, their great objection to the act of security is that it will be noe security, because by a clause in it the Government being in effect dissolved in the case of her Ma^{ty} death, the convention will be a Mobb or a polish dyet, which no man will come to but he that trusts to his sabre. Now, this is true and solid and unanswerable were this nation to depend upon an act of security; but her Ma^{ty} and all her good subjects, being of a mind that they are not to depend upon it but to proceed to a nomination, it is obvious that her Ma^{ty} cannot doe better then to connive at this clause, for thus all men, when they are cool, will be convinced that the act of security is indeed noe security at all, and so, notwithstanding of it, will see the necessity of a nomination.

I am,

&c.

J. JOHNSTOUN.

fol. 126.]

Edinburgh, August 3^{d},
1704.

MY LORD,

I have the honour of yours about the act of Exclusion, which I my self was so much for at my first coming hither that I engaged to the D. of Argile and my Lord Annandale to be for it, and it's like, had we been early with it, it had done good and answered the obvious reasons for it. But now we cannot carry it, nor come near to carry it. The Jacobites will be all against it, and the well meaning men too that join with them, because, say they, it will spoill the Treaty, it being a yeilding of the half of the subject of it. Then, say the Limitation men, if an Exclusion be past, we shall never have Limitations; for the Nation will have an act of Security, and an act of Security with an act of Exclusion will indeed render the nation so secure that we shall have no Nomination in her Maj^{ts} lifetime, & consequently no Limitations but confusion and violence. Besides it's a notion received here by the imprudence of the Emissaries of Hannover that that Court is ag$\overline{t}$ Limitations, and, therfore, say the Limitation men, Hannover and all their dependants, incase of an act of Exclusion, will rather take their chance of a Nomination without Limitations upon her Maj^{ts} death than have it in her lifetime with Limitations. Add to all this that, supposing the Duke of Queensbery & his freinds put all their strenth to carry this act of Exclusion, as I have ground to beleive they will, to recover themselves with the country here, yet this would signifie very litle, for a great part of his strenth is downright Jacobite, and will never be for an Exclusion. Nay, men of the greatest interest and best quality amongst them own that he has not used them as gentlemen if ever he pretended to the Queen that they would be for the Succession, for he knew the contrary.

The Earle of Marchmont moved for an act of Exclusion twice and was scarcely seconded, but his design was not to push it but to fright the Jacobits into a Cess, and which he did by concert. But he allowes me to writ that he thinks it the most inadvisable step that can be made to push it at present. The Advocat, too, who was mightily for it, owns that it will not carry, but thinks that the pushing of it will make a great discovery to the Queen. But why a discovery to the Queen of that which is no secret to her and the discovery of which would only serve to give a disreputation to the state of her Maj^{ts} affairs here? Besides, tho it would appear a true discovery in England and elswhere, it would be indeed a false discovery; for it would make no discrimination betwixt Jacobit and no Jacobit, nor any breach at all betwixt the Jacobites and others that joine with them. The Advocat has now been with me and yeilds; but he is for passing the act impowering and naming Commissioners to Treat, hoping that good men may be gott named both amongst the Lords & Burroughs, or that the Nomination may be gott left to the Queen, neither of which I beleive; for he ownes they design to frustrate the Treaty. However, the time and place no doubt must be left to the Queen; ffor, if they persist that the Borders be the place, all is a Jest. I apprehend they'le be for naming the Commissioners by the whole parliament, and not by the three Estates severally, as is usuall. In that case they'le carry all the Commissioners because of the Superiority they have amongst the Burrous, and if so, considering matters only as they stand here, I know no reason to retract what I wrot formerly. But, that matter being subject to other views at London, no doubt the Commissioner will receive her Maj^{ts} orders about it. As to what yor Lōp writes of the consequences of the distance, had her Maj^{tie} been here, matters had gone according to her pleasure. Nay, had her Ma^{ty} been at York, they had gone quite otherwise than they have done. Nay, till the morning of the day in wch the Resolvs past, we were as sure of 96 as we could be and ther were but 200 present. The hopes of success by a Treaty turned mens heads on the suddain, and the heads of the opposition, who at first called a Treaty *damnation* (D: Hamilton's own word), finding they would have no Majority without it, called it *Salvation* in the parliament, if I mistake not. I hope I have your Lōps permission to use another hand.

I am,

&c.

J. JOHNSTOUN.

fol. 128.]

MY LORD,

I reckon the session now over whenever her Ma^{ty} pleases, and I beg leave to write of my self. I told My Ld Marlborough that I would rather goe and attacke the lines with him then doe what I have done, and yet I knew not the half of my work. However, it seems I knew as much as ought to have made me wiser then to have taken the load of this bussiness upon me by coming singly into a post at this tyme. My only temptation was that it seemed not fair to have brought the Com^r into the fire and to leave him there alone, as I must have done since others declined posts; but, now, others

will take posts and my being here so long as the ferment
against me lasts can be of noe use. Then, tho I my self can
dispyse what I meet with, I would at least see my wife safe at
London, for here she cannot sleep sound, having had stones
threwn through the windows into her bed chamber big enough
to kill her, and without me she will not goe, being constantly
alarmed by the whispers of officious friends. I owe, too, at
London more money then my post (tho a good one) will pay
this year. I have yet one reason more. I would undeceive
your Lōp as to certain mistakes you are in with respect to this
nation and which I contributed to, being in them my self. I
have, too, letters from London that I have spoilled all with my
heat and cannot stand my ground, but I have directly nor
indirectly expressed noe heat here, if not once in part ags^t
M^r ffletsher for his impertinencys, and in my letters to your
Lōp against men not for their past but present behaviour.
But I reckon plain dealing acceptable to your Lōp; and noe
man here has done so much to unite people as I, as will appear.
However, as I am far from declining the honour of her Ma^{tys}
service; so, if any presents himself that will serve her Ma^{ty}
more faithfully, I am ready to make way, and to put in my
claime for a post, where my charge will be under Lock and
Key.

To trouble your Lōp noe more, I humbly beg that you will
interpose with the Queen not for an order for me to come to
London (her Ma^{ty} has done enough for me already), but for
Leave to come to it, which was the old frugal stile, and I shall
be at a point with the Com^r & Chan^r as to any thoughts
I have that concern the settlement of the Government before
I leave this place. I may ad that you will be rid of my
letters.

I am,
&c.
J. JOHNSTOUN.

Ed^r 6 Aug. 1704.

fol. 188.]

MY LORD,

You will forgive my concern for my friends, which is not whether they be in or out, but that they act upon this occasion so as to reconcile what they owe to the Queen and what they owe to themselves. If the present state of her Ma^{tys} affairs require their being out, still it will be noe disservice to her Ma^{ty} to reserve them for another state, for there will be more then one. Now, if this be the case and that their laying down will not be considerred undutifull, I beleive upon the least Intimation they will doe it. They have great reguards to your Lōp and will retain them thro out, but I own they have none for those, either here or there, whom they take to be their Governors at present. If your Lōp can put but a hundreth part of the confidence in me that they doe, I shall write to them, either as from you or from my self only, and I hope this matter will in due tyme have consequences that will shew it was good service done.

I am,

&c.

J. JOHNSTOUN.

Saterday, 5 May, 1705.

APPENDIX III

Letters of William Johnstone, 1st Marquis of Annandale, President of the Privy Council and Secretary of State in Scotland, to Godolphin.

Brit. Mus. Add. MSS. 28055.

fol. 156.]

MY LORD,

I have presumed this night to give her Majestie ane account of the parting thiss day off the Generall Assemblie.[1] In the whole progresse off these Proceedings there appeared the greatest dutie and affection to hir Majesties person and Interest, and there debaitts and affaires were managed with all due Regaird and respect to Her Majesties Authorittie and Government. They received from me the dissolution off this Assemblie and the Appointment off the next in her Majesties name and by hir Authorittie with all becomming Respect and submission, tho there were endeavors used (by some here who designe neither peace in Churche nor state) that itt should be otherwayes. I shall nott trouble your Lop: now by being particullar. I hope to have a more convenient oppurtunittie for this heerafter.

I kno nott how to tutche thiss unluckie affaire off the English shipps Crew, for the Character I have carried has keeped me from annie Intermedling in that matter, butt I must say, had all hir Majesties Servants acted that Vigorous and dutifull part that became them, the Insolencies and Irregularitties, spiritt and ferment off the People, had never come to annie highth, butt the appearance that was made in the first Instance against Her Majesties Commands transmitted by her Commissioner and the absenting off some off her Cheiffe

---

[1] Annandale was Royal Commissioner to the General Assembly.

Officers off State gave Life to this shamefull business, whiche ought to be detested and abhorred when itt is considered what appearances and Insults the Mobb were guiltie off upon this occasion such as has never been practised in my tyme nor for the age before in this nation.

I acknoledge the honor off your Lōps which I had some few dayes agoe. I wishe to receive your Commands and directions in what may concerne her Majesties Interest and Service here, for no man will more unbyassdlie and Impartiallie prosecute them, and I never shall minde either partie or Interest when Her Majesties measures and affairs call for my Assistance. Iff this is nott the rule, whiche I have too much reason to apprehend will nott be with mannie off Her Majesties servants, the success next session off Parliament will nott answere. I beg your Lōp Pardon for this tedious trouble and that you will beleive me with the greatest sincerittie,

My Lord,
&c.
ANNANDALE.
Holyrude houss, the 12th off Apr. [1705].

fol. 170.]

MY LORD,
Since My Ld Commissioner [Duke of Argyle] came to thiss Kingdom he has verrie fullie disscoursed some off Her Majestis servants annent the present Circumstances off her affairs and Government, and, I dare say, withoutt resentment or prejudice wee have honestlie given our opinnion, and what wee think is absolutelie necessare att thiss tyme for the true Interest off her Majesties Government and Authorittie, and successe off Her Majesties measures next session off Parliament. I have formerlie given itt of my oppinnion to your Los that itt was necessare the government were off a peece and unitte. I must now say, unless itt be soe, wee can have noe probabilittie off successe next session off Parliament, for the behaviour and

appearance off her Majesties servants who were last employed
has been soe gross and undutifull in thiss unluckie bussiness
off the English ships Crew, bothe towards her Majestie and
her Commissioner, that I can with no reason think they will
give annie manner off concurrence or assistance next session off
Parliament. I have no privat nor particullar veue off my
oune. Itt is my conviction and duettie to her Majestie and
her service and my zeall for a good understanding betwixt
these two nations that forces thiss freedome, and I doe assure
your Los: that all my appearances and actings shall ever be
suittable to this, for I think itt is our greatt and Important
Concerne att thiss tyme. I shall nott truble your Los: with
particullars, since My Ld Commissioner will give you ane
account of the unanimous opinnion off her Majesties
servants whom his Grace was pleased to Call and advise
with upon thiss occasion. I may say itt is given as the
onlie probable way to sett matters right heare, and to obtain
successe in her Majesties affairs, and I hope itt will be soe
received by Her Majestie. I shall never presume to give
advice butt with the greatest fidelittie and zeall for Her
Majesties honour and Interest, and soe, as I hope, your Los :
will beleive that I am with the greatest sincerittie,

My Lord,

&c.

ANNANDALE.

Holyrude Houss, the 26th Apr. [1705].

fol. 210]

MY LORD,

I kno these frequent adresses are uneasie, butt the
present juncture and necessittie off the Queens affaires, I hope,
will plead my excuse. The Queen, as I understand, will have
laid befor her by thiss Expresse a new measure, which is that
wee should forbeare pressing the settlement off the succession,
and onlie thiss session off Parliament endeavor a previous

treatie for the benefite off our Commerce and trade with England. Thiss was the measure the opposing partie and the enemmies off the succession took last parliament to defeatt itt, and itt will appeare surprizing eneugh iff the Queens servants and those who were soe much against itt last session shall be obliged to goe in to itt thiss. I am affrayed itt will look soe like dropping the succession heare for good and all that wee shall never be able again with annie countenance to take itt up. The great argument for thiss measure that I have heared is that those whom wee are to bring to our assistance will not goe in to the succession and therfor wee must take them where they will goe. Butt, since I am perfitelie sattisfied that most of those who will goe in to the treatie onlie doe itt because they kno itt setts the succession att a distance, and will in the event ruine all hopes off Establishing itt heare, I must beg leave to say that I can by no meanes give thiss advice, for I think itt can neither consist with the Queens honour, Interest, nor Securittie, and I am fullie persuaded the saiftie and peace off these nations depend upon a constant and vigorous pushing the succession upon all occasiones, for I doubt nothing butt that the Queen may order her affaires soe as what possablie may nott be done in one session off Parliament will be done in ane other, and, when thiss nation does see that thiss is what the Queen and her servants heare will have done, I shall nott much question butt that in a little tyme itt may cast the ballance upon the right side, and I am more and more confirmed off your Los: opinnion that whom itt may please or displease the rule ought to be to bring in a Majorittie to the Queens measure, and thiss I am convinced can onlie obtain successe att Last. Butt to suitt a measure to the Inclinations off some people heare is, I must say, regairding men more then endeavoring to doe what I understand the Queen soe much desires to be done. I am affrayed to be troublesome and shall nott insist. I have presumed to enclose by way of Memoriall for your Information some short reasons which may be more obvious that way then by way off letter. My Lord, I hope you will favorablie construct my concerne att thiss tyme, since I think the Queens service and Interest soe much att stake, for I doe solemnlie declaire I have no vewe butt to serve the Queen faithfullie in Conjunction with annie bodie that will doe soe, for I am nott, nor will ever be, off annie partie furder then the Queens honor and service and the securittie off her Government directs me. Therfor I doe, with greatt submission to her Majesties Judgement and to the duettie I shall alwayes most faithfullie pay her, send my poor thoghts on thiss occasion to your Los: to be laid before her Majesty that in all my apearances in her service I may exoner my selfe and be determined by her Commands and pleasure. I beg, My Lord, your Los: will use me with freedome, for no man desires more to be directed by you and with greater sinceritie to owne himselfe att all tymes,

My Lord,

&c.

ANNANDALE.

The first of June [1705].

Some obvious Reasons why the Succession is to be pressed next Sessions of Parl: and not a Treaty.

1⁰/ Itt is to be observed A Treaty is nott agreable to that zeall and concerne her Majesty hathe hitherto shouen for settleing the succession, bothe by her Letter to the Last session off Parliament and the Commissioners speeche to that Effect.

2⁰/ A Treaty will finde the same difficulties and oposition to the naming off Commissioners that the sucession itt selfe will.

3⁰/ The Conclusions off a Treaty, beeng to be reveued and canvassed by both Parliaments, will finde ass few frinds to aprove off them as the succession will att present finde for settling off it, becaus these Conclusions must pass in a Scots Parliament preciselie as England aproves them *et e Contra*, whiche seemes to have vast difficulties.

4⁰/ Itt is off greatter advantage to Insist upon the succession, becaus, tho itt should misscarry att thiss tyme, yett a Treaty may be taken up after, wheras, iff a Treaty miss-carry, I am affrayed there will be no place for the English succession.

5o/ The Act of securittie provides that the English successor shall be for ever excluded unless the Limitations be settled in a Scotts Parliament in the Queens Reigne, (whiche I pray God may be Long and Glorious), butt a Treaty, requiring necessarlie a tract off Long tyme, and whiche may be Industriouslie made Longer, leaves the nation too much exposed to the provision off that Law and to the affoording a handle for the Enemmies off the Protestant succession to debarr the English successor for ever even by the Expresse wordes off that Law.

6o/ A Treaty beeng the delay whiche was contrived last yeare for putting off the settling the succession by the then Ministry, the takeing itt up now seemes rather to be to fitt a measure for the Ministry then to fitt a Ministry for the Queens Measure, becaus nothing off her Majesties service is promoted by thiss change.

7o/ The Treaty looks too like the sense off a speeche made by a Minister of State last Parliament that itt may be her Majesties revealed will to have the succession settled, butt her secrett will itt should nott be acomplished, whiche might be to expose her Majesties naturall Candor and honor to the worst off People who durst venture to give itt such a turne.

June 1 [1705].

fol. 240.]

3ᵈ off July [1705]

May itt Please your Majestie,

I am ashamed to give your Majestie annie truble aboutt what may be off less concerne when wee have now affairs off the greatest consequence ammongst us, butt what I presume to lay befor you is what I humblie conceive to be the right off the office I have the honor to serve you in, and

wheroff the President off your Councill has been in possession
ever since the Revolution, as I doe evince by the Memoriall
I presume to transmitt to your Majestie by his Grace My
Lord Commissioner. I pretend to nothing butt to maintain
the authorittie and respect that is due to your President off
your Councill and to use that and all the Interest I have in
the world faithfullie in your Majesties service.

I hope your Majestie will pardon me that I am forced to
say, never was there more occasion for zeal and vigor in your
service then now, for the opposers are bold and obstinatt.
Yett I am verrie hopefull that in a little tyme, by the faithfull
conduct and prudent zeal off My Lord Commissioner and the
assistance off your servants heare, who concurr with him and
will support him in your service, thiss session off Parliament
shall be brought by a considerable pluralittie to a happy issue
and all your affairs and publick business off thiss nation shal
be finished to the sattisfaction off your Majestie and all your
good subjects. By what I presume to lay befor your Majestie
I design onlie to maintain the respect that is due to your
President off your Councill. Were itt a personall Interest off
my oune, I should nott have presumed to have given your
Majestie annie truble, butt, itt beeng the concerne off the
Character, Your Majestie will graciouslie endulge me your
pardon for laying itt befor you, for, as my life and fortune and
all I have in the world shall ever be zealoussie and faithfullie
employed in your service, soe I doe most dutifullie subject my
selfe in thiss as in evrie other thing to your Majesties commands
and shall ever, with the greattest duettie and sincerittie, give
prooffs that I am,

May itt please your Majestie,
&c.
Annandale.

fol. 242.]

My Lord,

I presume by thiss truble to aske the favor off your Loss:
that youl allow the secrettarie deputt for Scottland to reade

a Memoriall to you relaitting to a peece off respect that has been in use to be payed to the President off the Councill heare and whiche is now disputed by My Lord Chancellor [Earl of Seafield]. I shall nott truble your Los : to repeatt or say annie thing off itt heare. The Memoriall is full and I hope will sattisfie your Los itt is true matter off fact which will nott be contraverted by annie. I oune I am ashamed to give your Los : thiss truble since itt was my misfortune to faile off many occasions I sought for when att London to have had the honor off discoursing with your Los : the Queens affairs and hir publick business in thiss nation. I shall onlie say now, My Lord, none shall serve hir Majestie with greatter zeall and fidelittie then I shall doe and there never was more occasion for itt, for never was such projects and parties formed against hir Majestie government and Monarchie as now seeme to be, for there is a verrie obstinatt and avoued appearance and opposition to all hir business and to the peacable Issue off thiss session off Parliament. Yett I am verrie hopefull in a little tyme the loyle Conduct and faithfull Management off my Lord Commissioner [Argyle] shall overcome all difficulties and bring thiss Parliament to such a Conclusion as will be sattisfieng to hir Majestie and all hir good subjects.

The Memoriall I send hir Majestie is what concerns the office I have the honor to carrie and nott my selfe personallie, else I could nott have presumed to have trubled your Los : with itt. I shall beg your favor and assistance, and, iff your Los : can forgive thiss truble and allow me, when hir Majestie may be concerned, to renew itt, I shall use itt as one who considers your Los : off the most faithfull of hir servants ; and shall ever continue,

My Lord,

&c.

ANNANDALE.

Holyrude hous, the 3^d off July [1705].

MY LORD,

I am verrie loathe to truble your Los: unless I thinke
I have something worthe while. Yesterdays proceedings,
I think, determines the greatt affaire with us for thiss session
off Parliament. D: Hamilton did propose the enclosed resolve,
and backed itt with a Long speeche. He was seconded by the
D: of Atholl and mannie such. I was the first spoke in
oposition to itt as beeng a negative upon the succession and
contradictorie to the Measure proposed by the Queen. I
pressed much the inconvenience off Resolves, and the restraint
they were upon the Liberty and freedome off the proceedings
off Parl:, and was seconded by mannie. I thoght by thiss to
have baffled thiss business, and that itt was the fairest ground
to bring a Majorittie, since upon the sixth wee had by a Vott
preferred treating by overtures to Resolves, butt wee were
outt voted after itt came to the Vott, 'approve or nott' the
resolve, by fortie three. I shall nott truble your Los: att
present by beeng more particullar how the Vott and reasoning
went then to tell you that itt is the same resolve that was last
yeare oposed to those who then managed business for the
Queen, and that even they were ass much against itt now as
they were then, and I must say, iff others who are now
employed had performed there part, wee had throwen outt
thiss resolve, and consequentlie might have promised our
selves success in the settlement off the Succession whiche
I have ever understood to be her Majesties Measure. I hope
there will be supplies gott for the forces, and I see little more
to be done that will be for the Queens service or Interest thiss
session, for our business will be most now to keep them from
makeing entrenchments or invasions upon the Croun and
prerogative, whiche I am affrayed may bee too much designed
by those who may move the act for encreasing the representation off members for counties and some other proposalls off the
same natture. Iff such a treatie as may not be prejudiciall to
the settlement off the succession can be obtained, and the
nomination gott, soe as may be for the Queens honor and

interest, I shall be verrie glad to see itt, and shall assist with my endeavers that itt may be ass much to the Queens minde as possible, for, now that wee are putt by hopes off settling the succession thiss session off Parl:, wee must make the best off itt. I cannot be particullar with your Los : how thiss has misscaried att thiss distance. I must reserve itt to meetting ; then I hope your Los : will allow me to be plain. I onlie now tell you that the D. off Queens. frinds, my Ld Cromarties, my Ld. Stairsis, and my Ld. Registers frinds and mannie off the servants turning to the treatie has intyrlie defeated the setlement off the succession at thiss tyme. I humblie beg your Los : pardon for thiss truble and that I may kno from you the Queens minde and Commands upon thiss occasion, whiche shall ever be my rule in business.

I shall onlie add that the shorter our session off Parliament be now itt will be the more for the Queen and thiss nations Interest in my poor opinnion, butt all thiss with the greatest submission and regaird to her Majesties good will and pleasure, and I am ever with the greatest faithfullness,

My Lord,

&c.

ANNANDALE.

Holyrude houss, the 8th off July [1705].

The Marquesse off Lothian, married to the Commissioners Aunt, Voted for the resolve, and the Marquiss off Montrose declaired himself for the succession on Limitations and Voted against itt.

fol. 257.]

MY LORD,

I have nott trubled your Los : since I came to thiss Kingdom, nott doubting you have full accounts off all matters from other hands. I promised the Queen, and I told your Los att parting I wold doe my duetie in hir service and advance hir Majesties measures and Interest in thiss session off Parliament and upon all other occasions in thiss nation with my outtmost power and capacittie. Thiss I have done upon thiss emergent, and have a full and firme adherence off all my Frinds in hir service. Were itt necessare, I might call even my enemmies themselves to wittness my appearance upon thiss occasion and that bothe my Frinds and I have acted our parts. I pretend to no meritt, for I have done no more then my dutie, beeng perfetelie convinced and sattisfied that thiss nation can never be happie, nor our Religious and Civill Interests secure untill the same succession with England be the settled succession heare. What I doe is upon principle and Inclination, and therfor no man shall outtdoe me in zeall and vigor in hir Majesties service, for to serve hir and support hir Authorittie and Government is our solid securittie, and chearfullie to comply with all hir demands and proposalls is to sett our selves upon the best foott and foundation. Had all hir Majesties servants thoght soe att thiss tyme and acted accordinglie and the frinds off those who have been off laitt laid asside from hir Government had nott joined the opposing partie, the successe had been to hir desire. I doe nott presume to truble your Los: with particullars, since I suppose you will have them from others. I shall ever continue in my dutie to serve hir Majestie, and, iff I erre, itt shall be by nott knoing hir will and Commands, for I must take nottice to your Los: that I am nott treated by my Lord Commissioner with that confidence and trust in the publick concernes that my forwardness in hir Majesties service and the share I have off the Government entitles me to. I doe tresspass and I humblie beg pardon. Yett I must take leave to give your Los: all joye off the honors the Queen has conferred upon you. I shall allwayes think they can never be with the same justice and Meritt bestoued upon annie other. I beg your Los: will favorablie receive thiss truble and beleive me to be with the greatest sincerittie,

My Lord,
&c.
ANNANDALE.

Holyrude houss, the 18th off July [1705].

fol. 259.]

The 21 off July [1705].

My Lord,

I hope your Los : will forgive me that I give you truble upon evrie thing that I think is off concerne and consequence to the Queens service and interest. I heare there is a signature passed hir Majesties hand in favors off the Lords off session for fifteen hundrethe pounds yearlie outt off a fund belonging to the toun off Eðr. The duettie off my office oblidges me to lett your Los : kno that itt is most Illegall, and, withoutt the toun off Eðr. consent, can never pass heare, and I doe assure your Los : the Magistrats and Communittie off the toune will never consent to itt. I have tryed and used my best endeavors with them in thiss matter butt to no purpose. Suche a signature att thiss tyme wold occasion more heatt and truble in the Parliament then I can expresse, and I doe assure your Los : wee need nothing to raise the ferment ammongst us.

I have att the desire off all the Magistrats and Communittie sent to Sir David Nairne a Memoriall against thiss signatture to be laid befor her Majesty, whiche was advised with her advocatt heare. I have alsoe sent the act off Parliament in there favors, whiche will sattisfie evrie bodie that thiss Imposition can be applyed to no other use butt for the payment off the debts off the toun off Eðr. withoutt there consent, and besides the Illegallittie off thiss I must say, my Lord, nothing could be more unseasonable then to dissoblidge, nay, I feare I may say, to loose the toun off Eðr. who have the greatt leading and influence upon one off the Estaits off Parliament, the Royall Burroughs, and soe unadvertentlie has thiss signature been sent that the Provist off Eðr. was never spoke to in the matter, soe that, My Lord, I must say, to pass such a signature in thiss way and maner might be off verie bad consequence to the Queens service heare, for upon all occasions the Magistrats and Communittie off the toun off Edr. are most usefull and assistant to the Government in the Queens service. My Lord, I have no other vewe in thiss matter butt the Queens Interest and service, and I am convinced, had itt been duelie considered, such a signature had never been offered. I onlie beg upon the Queens account that annie thing off thiss kinde may be stopt untill she heare her servants upon itt, for bothe her justice and interest is concerned to a greatt degree in thiss matter. My Lord, you will forgive me that I use freedome when I think the Queens service and interest concerned, for that shall ever be my principall vewe in all the affaires off thiss nation, and I shall ever desire that your Los will beleive that I am with greatt sincerittie,

My Lord,

&c.

ANNANDALE.

fol. 288.]

The 26th off August [1705].

MY LORD,

I have with others off her Majesties servants, att my Lord Commissioners desire, signed ane opinnion to her Majestie for giving the Royall assent to ane Act for encuraging the fisherie, and to ane act for a Commission off trade. The first will Impaire the revenue, butt how farr itt may goe tyme will onlie shoe, for noe bodie can certainlie determine thatt att present. The other seemes to be Callcullatte for derogating from Authorittie, and takeing the ordinarie pouers and business outt off the Queen and the Governments hands, for itt is a noveltie and never formerlie practised by Act off Parliament heare. I opposed bothe with all my arte in Parliament and voted against bothe, soe that I onlie give my opinnion with all submission for passing them upon the supposittion that wee cannot have the lesse and treatie, or the less by itt selfe, withoutt they have the Royal Assent. I cannot, indeed, My Lord, be positive att present whither even upon passing these Votts wee shall have the treatie such as the Queen will pass, and the lesse or either off them, butt sure I am, iff wee have nott, itt will nott be thoght the Queens interest to pass annie off thes Vots into Laws. I have used my outtmost endeavors to advance the treatie in such a Manner as may be agreable to her Majestie, butt I am affrayed eneugh itt may be Clogged soe as itt will nott answere, for wee were forced to part last parliament day withoutt beeng able to procure a first reading, for the opposing partie insist with great vigor and warmthe to have itt burthened with the repeating the prohibittorie Clauses in the English Act befor the Commencement off annie treatie. Her Majestie and, I hope, your Los : will believe that I shall continue to doe my part that thiss Affaire and all others in this session off Parliament may be concluded to her sattisfaction and for securing a good understanding betwixt the two nations, which I am affrayed is other wayes designed by mannie ammongst us att present.

I wishe wee had the supplies, but wee are now fixed that, untill the treatie and trade relaiting therto be concluded, the Act off supplie is nott to have a second reading. I am verie sensible itt should be off the worst consequence to the Queens interest and the Quiett and peace off thiss nation should the Parliament part withoutt giving supplies, which was the onlie mottive to me for signing the opinnion to her Majestie. Butt off two evills wee must allwayes choose the least, and I am heartillie sorrie that the Queen should be putt to suche a straitt, and I wishe, even when itt is granted, itt may doe the business. Iff wee have nott the Assistance off those who were last employed, itt will nott doe, for wee have carried nothing that has been favorable yett butt by there help and concurrence. I wishe a happie and a speedie issue to thiss Parliament. I shall make itt my greatt concerne that itt be ass much for the Queens honor and interest as can be. Soe soon as itt is over, I hope the Queen will allow me to Attend her as itt is my duettie and as my post and office calls me to, and that I may pay my respects to your Los with the sincerittie off,

My Lord, your Los : most

&c.

ANNANDALE.

fol. 298.]

My Lord,

Wee have yesterday in Parliament Voted a plain Act off treatie, and att the same tyme declaired that the treatie shall nott commence untill the Clause in the Englishe Act declairing us Aliens shall be repealed. The struggle was to keep thiss outt off the Act, whiche wee carried onlie by three Votts, having bothe the Dukes off Hamilton, Atholl, and all there partie with all those who were last employed in oposition to us. I am sorrie wee have thiss Clogg. I used my endeavors against itt. I wishe with all my heart wee had trusted to a plain Act off Treatie. Had the partie who were last employed acted the part they did (as I wrote to your Los :) in some former Votts, whiche wee carried, wee should have been able to have dropt thiss Clause Intyrlie. The houss have nott yett agreed whither thiss shall be by Adress, Instruction, or seperatt Act. Thiss will be part off next dayes work, and, as I can judge, will be either by Adress or Instruction to the Commissioners, who are left to be named by her Majestie. I hope in two or three dayes wee may have the necessarie suplies for the Forces, and then I must think that itt may be assweell for the interest off the Queens service as for the good off thiss nation that thiss session were ass soon att ane end as her Majestie pleases. I am with greatt truthe,

My Lord,

&c.

ANNANDALE.

Holyrude houss, the 2ᵈ off Sept.

APPENDIX IV

Portland MSS., Hist. MSS. Com., vol. v, p. 114.

IN the following letter from the Earl of Glasgow to the Earl of Oxford we have an explicit statement regarding the money sent from England to Scotland in connexion with the Union Parliament:

' 1711, November 22, Edinburgh.—I received a letter from the Commissioner for the public accounts desiring me to exhibit to them a true account of what public money was lent by the Treasury of England to the Treasury of Scotland from the month of May 1706 to the month of May 1707. Now there was no money lent by the Treasury of England to the Treasury of Scotland, & not the least vestige of it to be seen in the Treasury of Scotland, for if it had been known that there had been a farthing sent from England to Scotland it would have totally disappointed the carrying on of the Union. But, in respect that the fund for maintaining the Civil List was entirely exhausted by the charge of former Parliaments, her Majesty was pleased to order the Earl of Godolphin to remit twenty thousand pounds sterling to the Duke of Queensberry, Commissioner to the Union Parliament, to defray his charge as Commissioner & to pay some part of the arrears of her Majesty's Ministers that were resting preceding the Union Parliament & to pay some part to those that had Letters of Pension from her Majesty. Accordingly the Earl of Godolphin put twenty thousand pounds sterling in the hands of Sir David Nairn, Secretary Deputy, who remitted the said money to me who was ordered by the Duke of Queensberry to keep the account of the same & to disburse it by his Grace's order. This is the true matter of fact, & I being enjoined to carry on this matter with the greatest secrecy & privacy, for if ever it had been in

the least discovered during the "haill" session of the Union
Parliament, the Union had certainly broken, & I had been
infallibly "De Witted", I have judged myself in duty bound to
your Lordship to lay the account of the expending of that twenty
thousand pounds before you, & if you shall think it proper for
me to exhibit the same before the Commissioners for the
public accounts your Lordship will be pleased to let me have
your commands, which I shall punctually obey ; for the Commissioners desire a particular account from me upon the 20th
of December next . . .'

APPENDIX V

Letter of Earl of Mar to Messrs. Wisheart, Carstares, and Mitchell, ministers.

State Papers, Scotland, Letter Books, vol. i, p. 37, No. 24.

Whitehall, March 27th 1714.

GENTLEMEN,

I had the favour of a letter from you yesterday without a date, putting me in mind of the Assembly which is appointed to meet the 6^t of May. I have the good fortune to be known to some of you long, and I hope non of you will doubt of my doing all I am capable of in the station the Queen has been pleased to put me for her service, and for the good & quiet of my Countrey, which I know you all three have a very great concern for.

The Queen has been ever so indulgent & favourable to the Church of Scotland that all its members have very good reason to be sensible of it, and, as long as they behave sutable to the favours her Mat^{ie} has showen, I am perswaded she will continue you her protection and her care of its concerns.

But allow me, at the same time, to tell you that the accounts we have from Scotland of the behaviour of some of your Brethren for some time past in stiring up jealousies in the Peoples minds, as if their liberty's and rights, Religious and Civil, were in danger under her Mat^{ies} Administration, and encourageing them to buy up arms, and put themselves in a posture of defence looks very odd from Ministers of the Gospel who have had so great proofs of the Queens favour and whose duty it is to preach peace and obedience to her.

I would fain hope that there is not so much ground for these accounts as some people wou'd have us here believe. And what may be in it I perswade myself that it is contrar to your advice and opinion, but haveing this opportunity I could not but take notice of it, which I assure you is well meant towards you.

The Queen is the great Blessing of these Kingdoms; God preserve her long to us, and may all her subjects be sensible of the blessings wee enjoy under her Administration. Where have we any safety if she be disturbed?

I shall take care to put the Queen in mind of the approach of the Assembly, and make no doubt but her Matie will send one to represent her there who will be agreeable to you and will be with you soon.

I shall alwayes be glad of an opportunity of showing you how much I am,

Gentlemen,

Your most humble Servant,

MAR.

INDEX